THE
COLLECTED
TABLETOP

For my great friend Bitsy ~
Happy Collecting and
Entertaining !
Enjoy,
Kathy

THE
COLLECTED
TABLETOP

Inspirations *for* Creative Entertaining

KATHRYN CRISP GREELEY

with Heather A. Anderson

Photography by

J. WEILAND

GREENLEAF
BOOK GROUP PRESS

Published by Greenleaf Book Group Press
Austin, Texas
www.gbgpress.com

Distributed by Greenleaf Book Group LLC

For ordering information or special discounts for bulk purchases, please contact
Greenleaf Book Group LLC at PO Box 91869, Austin, TX 78709, 512.891.6100.

Design and composition by Greenleaf Book Group LLC
Cover design by Greenleaf Book Group LLC
Photography by J. Weiland

Publisher's Cataloging-In-Publication Data
(Prepared by The Donohue Group, Inc.)
Greeley, Kathryn Crisp.
The collected tabletop : inspirations for creative entertaining / Kathryn Crisp
Greeley ; written with Heather A. Anderson ; photography by J. Weiland. -- 1st ed.
        p. : col. ill. ; cm.
ISBN: 978-1-60832-155-1
1. Table setting and decoration. 2. Party decorations. 3. Entertaining. I. Anderson,
Heather A. II. Weiland, J. (Henry J.) III. Title.
TX879 .G74 2011
642.8   2011925952
ISBN 13: 978-1-60832-155-1

Part of the Tree Neutral® program, which offsets the number of trees consumed in
the production and printing of this book by taking proactive steps, such as planting trees
in direct proportion to the number of trees used: www.treeneutral.com

TreeNeutral

Printed in Canada on acid-free paper

11 12 13 14 15 16   10 9 8 7 6 5 4 3 2 1

First Edition

DEDICATION

This book is dedicated to two people who have supported, encouraged, and inspired me to follow my dream and write this book.

To my mother, Margaret Crisp Stratton, who has always taught me, "If you believe you can do it, you can do it!" Mother is my greatest mentor in my appreciation for lovely antiques and beautiful tablescapes. Her graciousness, gratitude, and faithful optimism have taught me so much about life and about entertaining. Thank you, Mother, for all of the self-confidence you have instilled in me.

To my husband, Wells Greeley, who is the love of my life and constantly supports my hopes and dreams. Wells loves to entertain at Chestnut Cottage and encourages me in all of my endeavors. His patience, understanding, and support have made this book a reality.

CONTENTS

ACKNOWLEDGMENTS

At Kathryn Greeley Designs we believe that every project takes a team to be successful, and this book is no exception! My staff has been so supportive, and I am very grateful for all of their assistance and patience.

I can never begin to show my gratitude to my photographer, J. Weiland. We have been a team from the very start, and I thank you, J., for your sense of humor, patience, hard work, and great ability. You are the best, and this book would not have been possible without you. You inspired me and encouraged me all along the way, many times when I thought that I could not work through another photo shoot.

To Heather Anderson, thank you for forming my rambling thoughts and ideas into readable text. And thank you for turning research and editing into a fun and creative process; I couldn't have done it without you.

I am so very blessed, and one of my truest blessings is my friend Ed Springs. It is a real gift to have such a talented friend like Ed, who so lovingly and graciously painted each of the watercolors in this book. That was certainly a labor of love and I thank you, Ed, from the bottom of my heart.

And to Julia Molloy and Tobi Fairley, thank you for your encouragement to get started on this book and follow my dream. And to my amazing client, Margaret Roberts, thank you for the lovely watercolor of Chestnut Cottage.

A few years ago, I had the good fortune to discover Archivia Books while wandering down Lexington Avenue in New York City. It seems that I made instant friends with the store's owner, Cynthia Conigliaro, and her assistant, Will Rogers. From the moment I mentioned that I had a dream of creating a book on entertaining, Cynthia has been supportive and helpful. She has taken me under her wing and given me the gift of her expert advice and professionalism. Thanks to Cynthia and her assistant, Will!

Thank you to all my clients who have allowed me to assist them with not only their design work but also their entertaining. And a special thank you to the clients who so generously allowed me to invade their homes and photograph for this book: Fred and Annette Anderson, Mike and Holli Morris, George and Dodie Ragsdale, Mitch and Sue Levine, Ed Springs and Bo Henderson, Ron and Laura Leatherwood, and a special couple who wish to remain anonymous.

Thank you to all the antique dealers who loaned me anything I asked for, especially all of my friends at Village Antiques. And I have been so humbled by the generosity of Replacements and the gift of my new friend there, Sandra Jones, who has shown me treasures I never knew existed. Thanks to Brad at Mud Dabber's Pottery for creating the lovely set of pottery dinnerware just for this book. Annette Lewis at the Baggie Goose helped me immensely by suggesting many creative options for all of the event invitations. I appreciate your delivery—often almost overnight—and that you never said, "We can't"! A big thanks to my energetic friend Diana Laursen at the Hazelwood Soap Company for all of her fabulous creations. Thanks to Sally and Steve Eason, owners of Sunburst Trout Company, for their great foods for entertaining. Thank you to my long-time friend Angie Robinson Mallonee for assisting me in editing the recipes, and to Randy Cunningham, for the use of his gorgeous wooden boat. And thanks to Elizabeth Galecke, of Elizabeth Galecke Photography, for my personal photograph.

And did I luck out when I fell into the hands of Greenleaf Book Group! Thanks so much to Tanya Hall for her enthusiasm for my book and her TLC! And thanks to each member of my team at Greenleaf for your special talents and support.

And most important, thank you Wells for your constant support and encouragement and for tolerating Chestnut Cottage being turned upside down for several photo shoots. Most of all, thank you for believing in me.

INTRODUCTION

I believe that one of the greatest gifts we can give family and friends is memories. Sharing one's home by creating memorable events is a wonderful gift for guests and should be a great joy to those who put their energy into entertaining. As an interior designer, I place a great value on creating lifestyles as well as simply designing interiors. Our homes should be our havens, away from the busy and stressful world. My design philosophy has always been that a home should be collected, not decorated. The items that are a part of your home must have a connection to your life and tell your story. Perhaps you enjoy collecting antiques, or maybe art glass stirs your passion. Incorporating your collections into your life means using them creatively and sharing them with family and friends.

This book is about my passion for collecting and designing tablescapes. Tabletop collections can soften the hard edges of our busy lives and add beauty and quality to everyday dining as well as special occasions. Mixing antique collections with contemporary tabletop pieces adds drama and a sense of the unexpected. The juxtaposition of the grand and opulent with the ordinary and humble, and the intermingling of a variety of colors and textures add interest to tabletop design. Buy what you love, and buy the very best you can afford when building your collections—and use them! And please, do not mistake my use of the word "collection" to suggest the rare and precious. I believe that nothing is too precious to be used.

Collections always have a history. Perhaps your antique china was used in an English country house by several generations, or maybe your hand-thrown pottery collection was

Collecting and entertaining are rituals, and memorable entertaining and tabletop designs help to establish traditions in our lives.

recently made by a third-generation potter. Your collected tabletop may have belonged to your great-grandmother, or you may have found a beautiful collection in a vintage shop that really "spoke" to you. Collecting and entertaining are rituals, and memorable entertaining and tabletop designs help to establish traditions in our lives.

Every piece that I have collected through the years evokes memories of the place I found it. I have long been an avid collector of antiques, and I have spent years of weekends trawling in antique shops and at auctions, fairs, and markets. My career as an interior designer has also allowed me the joy of starting collections for clients—antique flow blue, majolica, art glass, pottery, even quilt collections. This has fueled my creativity.

Reserving your collections just for special entertaining events is truly a shame. Enjoy them daily. A designer friend of mine always says, "Life is not a dress rehearsal." This applies to using and enjoying your collections no matter their age or value. I have collected Flow Blue china for many years, and I use it daily. Most antiques were used before they found a home in our collections, and they will mellow with age as they are loved and used by us. Plus, don't you think that antique tabletop collections could certainly be considered the ultimate recycling effort?

Most every home has a personality, and I believe that some homes truly have a "soul." Most of the entertaining that I do for family, friends, and clients occurs at my home, Chestnut Cottage. I must tell you about Chestnut Cottage so that you can fully understand my passion for entertaining. Fortunately, about twenty-five years ago, I found a tiny nine hundred-square-foot cottage, and it was love at first sight! This cottage definitely had a "soul"; I felt it as soon as I crossed the threshold. I instantly had a vision of a pretty English cottage surrounded by English cottage gardens. I adored everything about it—the warmth of the wormy chestnut wood, all the little nooks and crannies, but above all else, the sense of belonging that I felt in every room. And anything that has a soul and a personality must have a name. I was single at the time, and the day I purchased the cottage, I named it Chestnut Cottage.

After my marriage to Wells Greeley, we made two additions to the structure, being very careful to retain its cottage feel. The main addition was added for more entertaining space. An enlarged kitchen and the addition of a gathering room have given us additional room for entertaining, not to mention new places for more collections!

My passion for collecting and entertaining has grown through the years, especially in my time at Chestnut Cottage. Large and small groups gather regularly at Chestnut Cottage and in its gardens for all sorts of events, from cozy dinners for four, to wine tasting events in the garden, to holiday fund-raisers for community organizations. Aside from my design

work, I spend most of my life in my large open kitchen, preparing for entertaining, or in my English-style cottage garden tending my perennials. I work in the garden, and it always rewards me with lovely flowers for our daily life and for our entertaining events.

Growing up, I loved eating at my paternal grandmother's home. She had Blue Willow dishes that most likely were purchased from the local five-and-dime. This grandmother was a true countrywoman, and she took great pride in both her vegetable and flower gardens. I suppose this was my start as a gardener and one who adores tending and arranging fresh flowers. At her home, I observed her love for cooking and providing casual day-to-day meals as well as extravagant holiday feasts for her large family. At my maternal grandmother's home, I was often "lovingly" reprimanded for making "mud pies" and serving these delicacies to my dolls and imaginary friends on lovely little tea sets.

In the 1950s, I observed my mother and her friends entertaining in a style that fascinated me. Each had interesting china patterns and tabletop collections. This inspired me even as a young child. Memories of Mother's bridge club parties are still fondly imprinted in my mind. When Mother's turn came to have bridge club at our home, I was always lurking in the shadows. I can still see Mother and her friends assemble for bridge club in their marvelous 1950s fashions and those to-die-for alligator stiletto heels, having a pre-bridge cocktail and smoking, which seemed extremely sophisticated to me at the time. I believe those observations of fashion and entertaining have greatly influenced my personal style.

I seem to have never outgrown this fascination and desire to entertain people in my home. From casual family meals to formal dinner parties, from old treasured recipes to brand new ones, nothing gives me more pleasure than creating memorable occasions for anyone who visits Chestnut Cottage. I have not collected antiques or any decorative pieces to be put away behind closed doors. Using each piece of every collection brings me joy. The thought of these lovely old pieces being locked away in a cabinet and never used would be heartbreaking. I love collecting, but most of all, I love using my collections. I urge you to use your collections—always! Why have collections if they stay hidden and you don't enjoy their beauty and usefulness? Tabletop collections give you endless opportunities for creativity. Whatever your entertaining style, start tabletop collections that reflect your personal taste and lifestyle. Using your collections creatively can create magic and a celebration at any meal.

Hopefully this book will inspire you to start a collection, or design one with family heirlooms, enjoyable antiques, or a variety of tabletop items such as china, glassware, cutlery, art glass, or pottery. These, combined with elements such as flowers, linens, and favors, unite to create memorable events. I want to share with you some of my tried-and-true recipes as well as ideas and inspirations for all types of entertaining occasions. Details such as invitation ideas, favors, flowers, and even some special styles of dining-room furnishings will inspire creativity in anyone who aspires to entertain elegantly. Color palettes were inspired by each collection and venue. Recipes were gathered from family and friends. Above all, graciousness should be the most outstanding characteristic of all entertaining. It is not about the expense of your tabletop collections; it is about the joy you will experience in collecting and sharing with family and friends.

I invite you now to come with me to Chestnut Cottage and several homes of clients and friends, and be a guest at twelve entertaining events as you experience many lovely tabletop collections.

Hopefully this book will inspire you to start a collection of family heirlooms, enjoyable antiques, or of tabletop items such as china, glassware, cutlery, glass, or pottery.

CHAPTER 1

BORDEAUX WINE TASTING DINNER

When our dear friends Fred and Annette Anderson announced their son Michael's upcoming wedding, my husband, Wells, and I planned a wine tasting to celebrate the occasion. Michael and his fiancée, Alison, had always shared an interest in wine, and they had attended wine classes and tastings since college. Their interest, together with our evolved wine cellar and Wells's recently acquired Bordeaux collection, suggested that a French Bordeaux tasting would be the perfect choice to celebrate their decision. We invited an intimate group of Michael and Alison's family and close friends to join in our celebration.

I have shared a longtime friendship and design relationship with Annette. We share many passions, and I have designed homes for her family at their main residence in Raleigh, North Carolina, a second home in Naples, Florida, and a beach home on the coast of North Carolina. Our friendship is one of my life's great treasures. I was honored when asked to design the floral arrangements for the wedding reception and was thrilled to open our home for this celebration.

The evening began in the wine cellar with champagne and hors d'oeuvres. Wells shared with our guests a few brief remarks on the history of French Bordeaux and an introduction to the wines they would be enjoying as the evening progressed.

Our wine cellar is in the basement of Chestnut Cottage, in a space that was originally a darkroom for the gentleman who built the home in the 1920s. The temperature and humidity make it the perfect place for a wine cellar. I had replaced an old porcelain sink with a copper one and fitted it into an antique French worktable. While designing the room, Wells and I had visited a multitude of wine merchants to request wine-box ends to display on the wall of the cellar. I serendipitously found a wallpaper depicting just that, which we hung on the cellar walls instead of the box ends.

Over many years, Wells has amassed quite a large assortment of antique wine accouterments, including a rare, French wine corker, and his collection is now displayed throughout the wine cellar. Also on display is one of his favorite bottles, Chateau Lafite Rothschild, 1982 Vintage, signed by renowned wine critic Robert Parker.

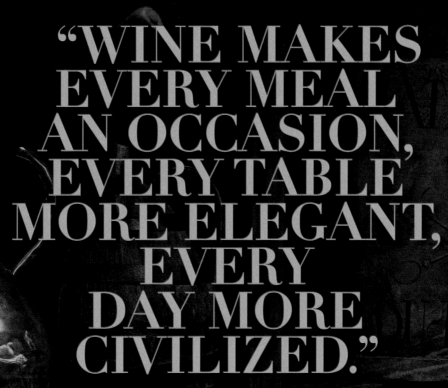

"WINE MAKES EVERY MEAL AN OCCASION, EVERY TABLE MORE ELEGANT, EVERY DAY MORE CIVILIZED."

—ANDRÉ SIMON

From the wine cellar, guests leisurely strolled outside to the sunken garden in the front yard of Chestnut Cottage, an ideal locale for summer dinner parties. Its grassy platform, defined by a stone wall and box hedges, sits alongside my rose garden. Old, bushy hydrangeas with bright white bundles offer privacy and lead guests down the stairs to our outdoor dining space. Massive boulders serve as steps leading from the front porch down into the sunken garden and also around the back of the cottage to the kitchen, making outdoor food service a breeze.

We had tables set up in the sunken garden for our evening meal and wine pairing. I chose a blue-and-white checked tablecloth and white linen napkins. The Old Coalport china sat beautifully on the blue and white. In each napkin, I tucked a bottle-shaped card I had designed with watercolors, which listed each course and wine pairing.

I mixed two of my crystal patterns—Waterford's Lismore and William Yeoward's Pearl—and at the insistence of my husband, added Riedel Bordeaux glasses. For place card holders, I made thin slits in wine corks Wells had saved for just such an occasion, and I placed each card in a cork. This subtle detail added a touch of the wine theme to the table.

I arranged full bouquets of hostas, casablanca lilies, peonies, coneflowers, roses, and delphiniums, as well as strategically placed candles in glass vases that were secured in tall metal bases. I wanted them to be high on the table so that guests could enjoy the rose garden and dinner conversation. I placed several cobalt blue votives below the tall arrangements for additional candlelight.

We arranged full bouquets of hostas, casablanca lilies, peonies, coneflowers, roses, and delphiniums.

WINE TASTING MENU

Wild Mushroom Phyllo
VACHERIN MONT D'OR

Veuve Clicquot Ponsardin Brut and Pol
Roger Cuvée Sir Winston Churchill 1995

Mache Salad with Goat Cheese-Stuffed Piquillo
CHATEAU COUSTAUT LA GRANGEOTTE 2009

Spinach- and Ricotta-Stuffed Shells
CHATEAU BELAIR PREMIER GRAND
CRU CLASSE 1995

Lemon Verbena Sorbet

Stuffed Tenderloin of Beef with Potatoes au Gratin
and Haricots Verts Bundles
CHATEAU LAFITE-ROTHSCHILD 1988

Crème Brûlée in Frozen Lavender Bowls
CHATEAU DUCLA EXPERIENCE XIV 2006

Classic French Cheese Tray
CHATEAU BEYCHEVELLE CLASSIC
GRAND VIN 2001

Mache Salad with Goat Cheese-Stuffed Piquillo

I also call this dish "Le Carré des Vosges Salad" because on a trip to Paris, I had this recipe at Le Carré des Vosges, a delightful restaurant tucked away behind the Place des Vosges in a beautiful seventeenth-century mansion. My traveling companion Annette Anderson and I are always "dissecting" dishes in restaurants, and I believe that we have this one almost perfect.

- Whole red piquillo peppers, roasted (found in gourmet specialty shops)
- Soft goat cheese
- Baby mache greens
- A good olive oil and a good champagne vinegar
- Prosciutto
- Shaved Parmesan
- Green olive slices
- Black olive slices
- Balsamic glaze

Stuff roasted piquillo peppers with a soft goat cheese. Toss mache greens in a light vinaigrette of olive oil and champagne vinegar. Place greens on a salad plate in a mound. Encircle the mache with a long slice of parma ham. Place two of the stuffed piquillo peppers on the plate. Top the salad with shaved Parmesan, and garnish the plate with a few green and black olive slices. Drizzle the salad with balsamic glaze.

Haricots Verts Bundles

This recipe is from one of my favorite cookbooks, Crème de Colorado, *published in 1987 by the Junior League of Denver. I have always found Junior League cookbooks to be among the best, and have made this recipe for dinner parties for years. This is a great side to assemble the day before and cook just before serving.*

- 2 pounds fresh green beans, steamed crisp-tender
- 6 strips bacon, partially cooked
- Garlic salt to taste
- 3 tablespoons light brown sugar
- 4 tablespoons melted butter

Gather 6–10 beans in a bundle and wrap each bundle with a strip of bacon. Secure the bacon with a wooden toothpick. Sprinkle each bundle with garlic salt and brown sugar. Drizzle the melted butter over each bundle and bake at 350 degrees for 15–20 minutes, until the bacon is done.

THE LEMON VERBENA
SORBET WAS SERVED
IN A GORGEOUS SET
OF ANTIQUE BOWLS
BY MOSER, CIRCA 1890.
THE INTAGLIO BOWLS
HAVE A QUATREFOIL
SHAPE AND SAUCERS
WITH BLOWN
FINISH PONTILS ON
THE BOTTOM.

We had created the evening's menu with the outdoor setting in mind, and we paired each course with a corresponding French wine. I reproduced a salad that Annette and I enjoyed on a recent trip to Paris: spring greens tossed in extra virgin olive oil, surrounded with prosciutto, topped with shaved Parmesan, and served with a side of piquillo peppers stuffed with local goat cheese.

The main course was a stuffed-beef tenderloin with green bean bundles and stacks of scalloped potatoes au gratin infused with rosemary from the herb garden at Chestnut Cottage. The bundles were created from fresh half-white runner green beans that I lightly steamed. I wrapped them into bundles with strips of lean bacon secured with toothpicks, dusted them with brown sugar and garlic salt, drizzled them with melted butter, and baked them in the oven. I made lemon verbena sorbet, which I served between courses in a gorgeous set of antique bowls by Moser, circa 1890. The intaglio bowls have a quatrefoil shape and saucers with blown finish pontils on the bottom. I purchased these exquisite bowls at Devonia Antiques in West Palm Beach and will use them for serving a variety of foods for years to come.

Classic Stirred Crème Brûlée

Makes six individual crème brûlées

- ✦ 8 egg yolks
- ✦ ½ cup sugar
- ✦ 2 cups heavy cream
- ✦ 1 whole vanilla bean split lengthwise
  or 1 teaspoon of pure vanilla extract
- ✦ 6 tablespoons superfine sugar for caramelizing the tops

In a large bowl whisk together egg yolks and ½ cup of sugar, until the mixture is thick and pale yellow. In a double boiler over simmering water, bring the cream to a gentle simmer. Remove from the heat and slowly pour into the egg mixture. Add the vanilla bean and pour the mixture back into the double boiler. Stir constantly over a low boil until the custard is thick enough to coat the back of a wooden spoon. This usually takes about 20–25 minutes. Remove the vanilla bean and chill completely. Serve in the ice bowls or in individual coffee cups. Top each with 1 tablespoon of superfine sugar and caramelize with a kitchen torch.

Crème Brûlée
in Lavender Bowls

This is a beautiful dessert that I had on a trip to Paris. The presentation is time consuming, but it will wow your guests!

✢ 2 glass bowls with a size difference of 2 inches (2 bowls per serving)

✢ Stems of lavender in bloom

✢ Water

✢ Masking tape

Place 3-4 stems of lavender in a circle around the bottom of the largest bowl. Place the smaller bowl inside the larger bowl, making sure that the smaller bowl is centered in the larger one. Using two strips of masking tape, secure the smaller bowl to the larger one by placing the strips of tape across the tops of both bowls. Fill the space between the two bowls with water, being careful not to let the water lap into the smaller bowl. Add 3-4 more stems of lavender to the water. Place the bowls in the freezer until frozen. Once the water is frozen, carefully slide the larger and smaller bowls off your ice bowl, running cold water over them if necessary.

Dessert was a delightful, stirred créme brûlée served in ice bowls with lavender from the garden frozen within, which made for a light, summery presentation.

After the meal, guests gathered on the upper porch for one last glass of wine and chocolate-covered strawberries as Michael and Alison opened their wine-inspired gifts.

Each guest left with a bottle of French Bordeaux in a wooden wine box scripted with *Cheers from the cellar of Wells Greeley*. This bottle would serve as a delicious memory of the evening and the celebration of this lovely young couple.

As our celebration ended, and dusk fell into darkness, the evening took on a magical feel with candlelight shining from the floral arrangements and wrought iron candelabras around the sunken garden. The perfect end to an enchanting evening!

OLD COALPORT, BY COALPORT CHINA

During a trip to Naples, Florida, while designing a second home for the parents of the groom, I discovered a small breakfast set of "Old Coalport," by Coalport China. This pattern, which I instantly fell in love with, features cobalt triple borders, gold leaf, and the bright color palette of unique floral sprays. Many of the flowers depicted in this pattern bloom in the garden of Chestnut Cottage. Each piece is marked with "Old Coalport Period 1825" in purple, and "Made in England, Coalport, A.D. 1750" and a royal crown in green.

Each couple left with a bottle of French Bordeaux in a wooden wine box scripted with "Cheers from the cellar of Wells Greeley."

This pattern was reproduced by Coalport China between 1979 and 1983 under the pattern name "Leighton Sprays." In my eyes, it is the most gorgeous floral china pattern I have ever owned. It is the detail in each and every piece that endears this pattern to me.

Over the years, I have continued to hunt and collect a variety of dinner, salad, and bread and butter plates, as well as cups and saucers. The team at Replacements, Ltd., have been invaluable to me in my search for pieces to add to this beloved collection.

Researching their listings indicates that Coalport China has several floral patterns called "Old Coalport." My collection is designated "Old Coalport (Gold Trim)." A bit of a mystery, but this always makes the "hunt" more fun!

Potatoes au Gratin

- 4 pounds Yukon Gold potatoes, sliced ¼- to ⅛-inch thick, unpeeled
- 2 onions sliced as thick as the potatoes
- 3 tablespoons unsalted butter
- 2½ cups heavy cream
- 2½ cups grated Gruyère cheese
- Salt and pepper to taste
- ¾ teaspoon freshly grated nutmeg

Preheat oven to 375 degrees. Spray a 9-inch × 13-inch baking dish with Pam. Place the sliced potatoes in a saucepan and cover with water. Cook only until slightly soft. Drain the potatoes. Saute the onion slices in the butter just until tender. Coat the bottom of the baking dish with a small amount of cream. Top with a layer of potato slices, then add a layer of the onion slices and a layer of ⅓ of the cheese. Pour ⅓ of the heavy cream over the layer and repeat with two more layers. Salt and pepper to taste. Slightly press each layer with a spatula. Sprinkle the nutmeg over the last layer. Bake for about 45 minutes, until bubbly and slightly brown on top.

I make the Potatoes au Gratin the day before I plan to serve them. When ready to serve, while cold, I cut circles with 3-inch tall by 2-inch round metal baking rings. The potatoes are easier to cut and remove from the baking dish when they are cold.

Place the potato rings on a baking sheet lined with foil. Heat until bubbly in a 375-degree oven. Use a spatula to remove the entire ring and place on a serving plate. Remove the ring and garnish the potatoes with a sprig of fresh rosemary.

As our celebration ended, the evening took on a magical feel with candlelight shining from the floral arrangements around the sunken garden. The perfect end to an enchanting evening!

In the garden next to my teapot topiary, Annette and I snuck a quiet breakfast the next morning and enjoyed the Leighton Spray breakfast set.

CHAPTER 2

A STUDY IN PINK

The delightfully pink cottage of my dear friend and client Dodie Ragsdale served as the perfect venue for this study in pink. Surrounded by pink roses, white hydrangeas, and a sweet white picket fence, this hideaway is nestled in the hills of Waynesville, North Carolina, and boasts breathtaking views of the Blue Ridge Mountains. I have worked with the Ragsdales for more than twenty years, and I delight in Dodie's love of pink and green. Decorating this home with Dodie was a joy, and planning this event only added to the special memories I have of the time I spent working with Dodie to make her "rose-colored" weekend cottage all that she envisioned.

Dodie's home certainly reflects my design philosophy of "collected, not decorated," with its mixture of new finds and old family antiques in her beloved palette of pink, green, and white. Kathryn Greeley Designs provided a custom-designed needlepoint rug with a green-on-green pattern and pink floral accents to harmonize with the fabrics and color concept throughout the house. The painted hollyhock-design botanical metal pieces on either side of the mantle were created by Chapel Hill, North Carolina, artist Tommy Mitchell.

WITH ITS NEW FINDS AND FAMILY ANTIQUES, DODIE'S HOME CERTAINLY REFLECTS MY DESIGN PHILOSOPHY OF "COLLECTED, NOT DECORATED."

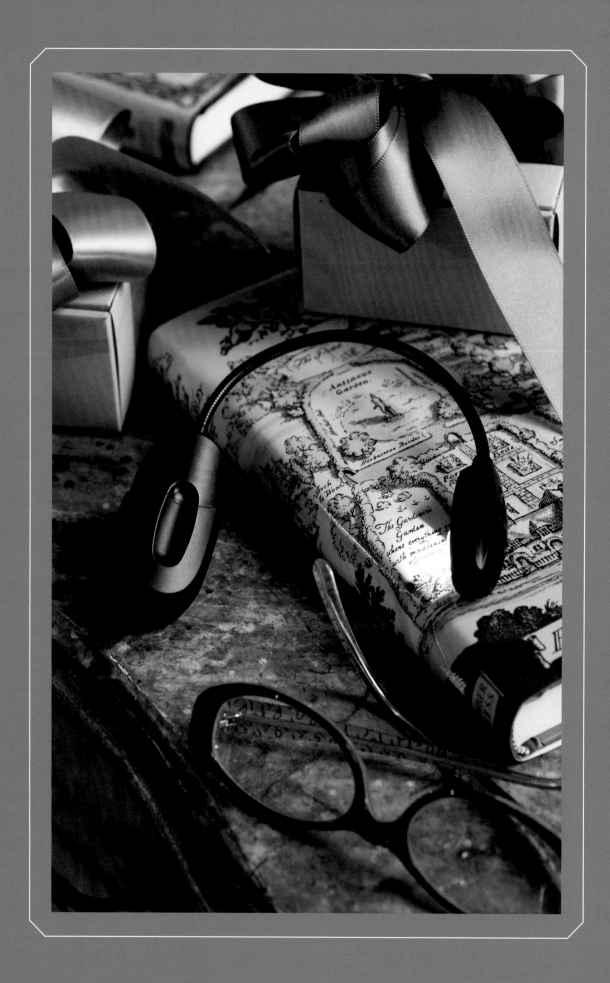

Down the Garden Path (1932)
A Thatched Roof (1933)
A Village in a Valley (1934)
How Does Your Garden Grow? (1935)
Green Grows the City (1939)
Merry Hall (1951)
Laughter on the Stairs (1953)
Sunlight on the Lawn (1956)
Garden Open Today (1963)
Forty Favourite Flowers (1964)
The Art of Flower Arrangement (1967)
Garden Open Tomorrow (1968)

Dodie and I share a love of gardens, and I wanted to introduce her to the gardening novels of Beverley Nichols. Nichols was a prolific writer, but he is best know for his rich, spirited stories of the homes and gardens he lived in throughout his life in England. He had a rare ability to bring life and humor to a subject often thought to be dry through his poetic writing style and his vibrant characters and descriptions. His books were out of print for many years and have only recently been reprinted by Timberline Press. I was overjoyed to discover several copies of the earlier editions in an antique bookshop in London. His gardening stories are full of practical information and inspiration for the passionate gardener, and I felt that a study of his works was the natural choice for a Book Club Luncheon at Dodie's lovely pink cottage in the hills.

I made the invitations from a combination of fine pink and gold-leaf paper and added a delicate pink flower. I added a simple turquoise ribbon to tie in the accent colors of the tabletop.

The focal point of this tabletop is undoubtedly the cranberry-shaded epergne, most likely English, from James Powell and Sons, circa 1880. Its fluted design perfectly featured Dodie's most beloved flower. The peony is known as the flower of prosperity and honor and is the embodiment of romance, compassion, and a happy marriage. Nothing could better represent Dodie and George's marriage. This flower holds such significance for Dodie that she was pleased to wait until the peonies of Chestnut Cottage, just down the road from her home, were blooming in all of their splendor. Any flower meaningful enough to dictate the season for such an event is worthy of only the most special presentation, and this unique epergne fit the bill.

Dodie's lovely antique dining table needed no tablecloth, so our tabletop setting began with white, linen drawn thread work place mats and napkins with delicate, embroidered pink rosebuds. I placed Luneville china dinner plates in the center of each mat, which perfectly showcased the pink and white dessert plates. The contrast between the rich pink and the bright white made this dessert service exceptional. Dodie's collection of silver flatware flanked the plates on all sides.

At the top of each place setting I positioned place card holders, circa 1920, that I discovered on an antiquing trip to Palm Beach, Florida. These intricately designed pieces feature gilded metal bases, most likely from Austria or Czechoslovakia, holding wonderful

I made the invitations from a combination of fine pink and gold-leaf paper and added a delicate pink flower.

Please Join Dodie Ragsdale

For

A Book Club Luncheon

to discover the joys of gardening

as told by author Beverley Nichols

on

Wednesday May 19, 2010

at

12:00 noon

138 Breezemont Drive

Please RSVP by May 10th

Menu

Rossini and Blue Cheese Wafers

A Salad Trio

Chicken - Broccoli Salad

Watermelon Summer Salad

Pasta Salad

Almond Mini Muffins
With Strawberry Butter

Individual Strawberry Tarts

*The peony is known as the
flower of prosperity and
honor, and is the embodiment
of romance, compassion, and
a happy marriage.*

turquoise etched-glass pieces, attributed to either Moser or Bohemian glass. As light darts through the turquoise glass, it reveals three young women dancing joyfully together, a fitting detail as friends gather to share mutual passions and fellowship.

I decided that functionality was the way to go with the favor for this event. Each guest received an LED book light for the nights when a book just cannot be put down. Those of us who enjoy reading have been asked many times to please turn the light off and go to bed. This favor was meant to be the ultimate solution for such predicaments. I wrapped the favors in a soft-pink box, tied a large bow from turquoise and green double-face satin ribbon, and placed the gift atop each guest's place setting.

In keeping with the theme of the event, I scribed the name of each guest in gold on bright-pink heavy paper. The Minton cups and saucers, with their feminine ribbon of turquoise, added a touch more of the accent color to the tabletop and sat just to the right of the place card holder. The pink juice glasses I found on the same antiquing trip

The image of young women dancing joyfully together is a fitting detail for a gathering of close friends.

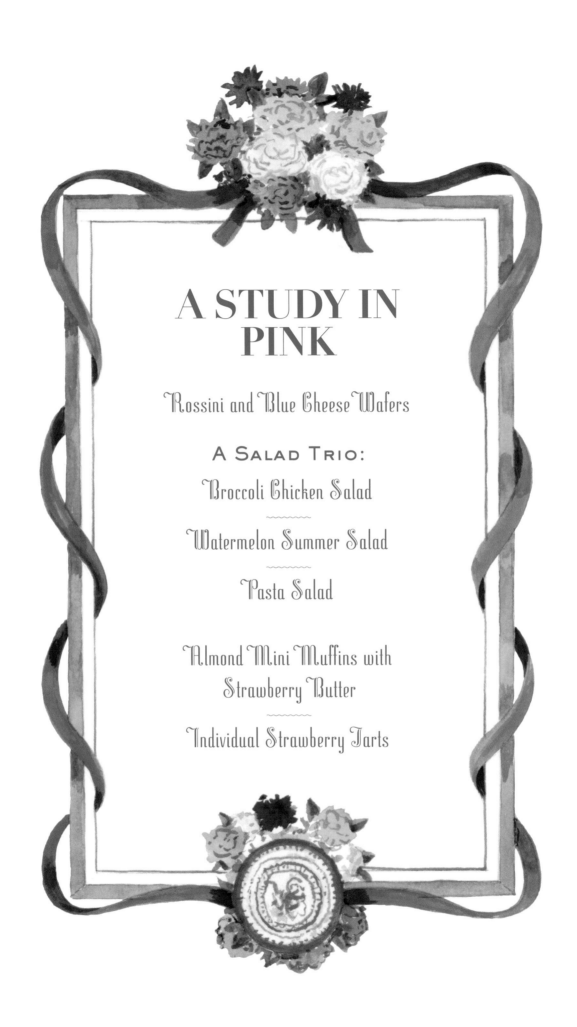

A STUDY IN PINK

Rossini and Blue Cheese Wafers

A Salad Trio:

Broccoli Chicken Salad

Watermelon Summer Salad

Pasta Salad

Almond Mini Muffins with
Strawberry Butter

Individual Strawberry Tarts

Watermelon Summer Salad

- 1 tablespoon balsamic glaze (available at gourmet shops)
- 1 tablespoon lime juice
- 2 tablespoons olive oil
- 2 tablespoons chopped fresh mint
- Sea salt and pepper
- 1 Sugar Baby watermelon, rind removed, seeded and cut into bite-sized chunks
- 1 red onion sliced into rings
- 4 ounces crumbled feta
- ½ cup sliced black olives

Combine the balsamic glaze and lime juice. Slowly whisk in the oil. Add the chopped mint and sea salt and pepper to taste. Combine the melon, onion, feta, and black olives. Slowly pour the dressing over the melon and gently toss until everything is lightly coated. Serve on individual salad plates and garnish with fresh mint.

Broccoli Chicken Salad

This recipe is great for ladies' luncheons and was given to me by my friend Annette Anderson.

- 4 boneless chicken breasts
- 4 cups water
- ½ cup light soy sauce
- 2 cloves minced garlic
- 1 (16-ounce) package fresh broccoli flowerets
- 4 green onions, chopped
- 1 cup dried cranberries
- ¼ cup toasted pecans
- Chutney Dressing (see recipe below)

Bring first four ingredients to a boil in a medium saucepan. Boil for fifteen minutes or until chicken is done. Drain, and when chicken is cool, cut into bite-sized pieces. Combine the chicken, broccoli, onions, cranberries, and pecans. Toss with the dressing until everything is well coated.

Chutney Dressing

- 1 jar of Major Grey's Chutney
- 1 cup Hellmann's mayonnaise
- 1 clove minced garlic
- ¼ teaspoon red pepper flakes

to Florida. Their elegant grape-leaf design was perfect for serving wine at a ladies' luncheon. I arranged pink and white old English roses from the gardens of Chestnut Cottage and Dodie's home in small crystal bud vases to add a touch of balance and complete the look of the tabletop.

With all the pink in the tabletop design, I thought a little pink on the plate would be appropriate. The salad trio included a juicy watermelon salad, and I added dried cranberries to the broccoli chicken salad for an extra touch of pink. Prior to lunch, guests were treated to an Italian *aperitivo*, Rossini, named in honor of the composer Gioachino Rossini. Similar to a Bellini, the Rossini substitutes fresh pureed strawberries for peach juice.

Of all the rooms that I have designed in this quaint little cottage, the kitchen must be my favorite. Crisp white cabinets and tongue-and-groove paneling contrast with the bright-pink and green antique plates that hang around the kitchen and the touches of lime green here and there. A large-scale pink and green floral print frames the window above a delightful window seat where one can read and enjoy the

sweet cottage garden. The back terrace is a great place to discuss the gardening stories of Beverley Nichols and have a fresh strawberry tart. Looking out over the beautiful mountains and pink and white roses, one might certainly feel transferred to rural England.

MYSTERIOUS COLLECTIONS

As a collector of china and other fine things, I relish uncovering the history and origins of the patterns I discover. Antique dealers and friends in the industry share information, and I discover facts through my own research. My library contains books dedicated to the gathering of such information and history, and I comb through collector sites on the Internet. Yet, even with the Web at my fingertips with its unlimited information, there are some pieces and patterns that will always remain a mystery. When all of my resources and experience in collecting and discovering have been exhausted, I find myself with an enigma on my hands. I am left with a beautiful pattern and little to no information or history. When this happens, there is nothing to do but enjoy and appreciate the beauty and aesthetics of such a pattern and enjoy contemplating the mystery it holds. These patterns become a special part of my collection.

Pink is not just a color. It's also an attitude, a way of life.

Sometimes, a china collection can be all that is needed to inspire an entire event, and in this case it was the delicate pink dessert set that I discovered at an antique shop in Western North Carolina. With no markings, it is a mysterious set, and I know only that its origins are English and that the contrast and depth of color in the pattern make it a rare and special find. The mystery only increased my appreciation of this collection, and it, along with the cottage, became the inspiration for A Study in Pink.

The other patterns I adorned this tabletop with are equally mysterious. The Luneville china pattern I used as the dinner plate, with its bright-white porcelain and pink, ribbon-like detail was made sometime during the nineteenth century. Luneville is a small town in Northeastern France that has been producing beautiful earthenware patterns since the mid 1700s.

My friends at Village Antiques in Asheville, North Carolina, loaned me the Luneville china and shared all of the information they were able to uncover. I have no pattern name or exact date of origin.

The Minton cups and saucers, circa 1910 England, added a touch of this event's accent color. Again, no pattern name, but the turquoise enamel ribbon, hand-painted flowers, and gilt trim definitely reflect the styles of Minton China of London, England.

CHAPTER 3

A GRANDMOTHER'S BOOK SHOWER

A sunny February day held the promise of an end to the grey skies of winter days and the first signs of the fresh, bright spring to come. Spring is a rebirth, and thus a fitting theme to celebrate the birth of a grandmother. This is the feeling I longed to share with the guests of Annette's Grandmother Shower.

Annette is an extraordinary woman, and her love for children is unparalleled by any I have ever witnessed. I often teased that she was a "grandmother wannabe." Once her wish was granted and she became a grandmother, it was time to celebrate. As a former first-grade teacher and a mother of three, she has always believed that books held the keys to expanding the minds and creativity of children. When my cohost, Anne Underwood, suggested a book shower, I knew it was the perfect idea. As an incurable collector, I immediately started the hunt for delightful antique children's books—and did I ever find some treasures!

With the invitation I wanted to convey to the guests what a special event this would be and give them just a hint of what lay ahead. For a creative touch I chose to design a bookmark rather than a standard invitation. Not only would it relay the theme of the event and add a personal touch, but it would also serve as a keepsake for Annette and her guests. I watercolored flowers in the likeness of the Mason's Ironstone Strathmore Blue pattern and attached a thin golden cord to complete the invitation.

THE KEEPING
ROOM OF
ANNETTE'S HOME
WAS DESIGNED
FOR THE SOLE
PURPOSE OF
BRINGING FRIENDS
AND FAMILY
TOGETHER.

The event took place in the keeping room of Annette's home, a room that I designed several years before for the sole purpose of bringing friends and family together. This conservatory-style room is absolutely ideal for entertaining and was designed with events such as this one in mind. It features two round tables for dining on one side and a comfortable seating area and wood-burning fireplace on the other. When designing this area, my intent was to keep it open and bright while also creating the illusion of two distinct spaces. We achieved this by placing an antique wooden library table, piled high with books, in the middle of the room. As a finishing touch, a large orchid arrangement stays nestled in an antique English footbath, circa 1870.

A clear view of the gardens and the sunlight beaming through the overhead roof lantern seem to transport guests to an English country home conservatory. The Pennsylvania Blue slate floors add to the natural element of the room. The flooring continues through the French doors to the outside, creating the illusion that the great room and the garden terrace are extensions of each other.

Hanging from the high ceilings are tremendous, hand-carved chandeliers that I commissioned from The Big Chandelier in Atlanta, Georgia, my top choice for antique lighting. These, along with recessed lighting, cove lighting, and antique sconces—all with dimmers—allow for customizable lighting options depending on the desired atmosphere.

One of Annette's favorite things is bringing loved ones together and serving up delicious meals, and she was thrilled with the idea of having two round dining tables rather than one large one. It makes

A view of the gardens transports guests to an English country home conservatory.

I knew the Strathmore Blue china would add a breath of spring to our luncheon.

for a more intimate dining experience and adds a wonderful aesthetic to the right room.

I reached out to my friend John Chapline, owner of First Circle in Oklahoma City, to help me create the tables and chairs I envisioned for Annette's keeping room. I have always been able to count on First Circle for the utmost dependability, incredible attention to detail, and craftsmen who work closely with designers to precisely achieve a desired style. The First Circle team consists of furniture designer John Chapline and five artisans, an ensemble of eighteenth-century souls in the twenty-first century with the rare ability to design and build enduring and endearing furniture. Be the project an antique reproduction or a new creation, First Circle strives for classic design lines without production lines.

Please join us for a
Grandmother's
Book Shower
and Luncheon
honoring
Annette Anderson
Saturday, February 20th
12:00 noon
100 Perquimans Drive ~ Raleigh
Given by
Kathy Greeley and
Ann Underwood
RSVP

The classic Regency style of this dining table is subtly enhanced with the addition of a custom thistle, vine, and leaf inlay. Delicate flowers strategically placed within the inlay add a feminine softness and accent the room beautifully. The primary wood of this table is walnut, and the inlay is a perfect combination of cherry, English oak, and rosewood. The First Circle armchair design is a contemporary interpretation of a Regency chair. The chair frame is walnut, and yew wood is used for the lovely curved back. I chose a striped upholstery fabric of green and rose with a touch of gold to add color and comfort to the design. These tables and chairs will be family heirlooms for generations to come.

Over the years, I have helped Annette build a significant collection of Mason's Ironstone Strathmore Blue china, and she was thrilled to let us use it for her shower. I knew it would add a breath of spring to our luncheon, so I created each floral arrangement and the table settings with this pattern in mind.

These tables and chairs will be family heirlooms for generations to come.

I wanted the floral centerpieces to look as if they had come out of an English perennial garden.

I began this tablescape with simple, white linen place mats, which looked spectacular atop the dark walnut table. Annette's Gorham silver in the Chantilly pattern lay on either side of the floral Strathmore Blue pattern. I placed the Royal Lace soup bowl and saucer on the dinner plate, making the pattern underneath all the more vibrant. Waterford's crystal Colleen water glasses and small vases made into place card holders sat at the head of every setting. Each guest enjoyed a small, personal floral arrangement with their name and a Strathmore Blue–inspired watercolor printed on a place card.

I wanted the floral centerpieces to look as if they had come out of an English perennial garden. I drew from the colors of the Ironstone pattern when selecting the flowers: blue and white hydrangeas; pink parrot tulips; dark blue delphiniums; pink and yellow roses; pink, white, and yellow lisianthus; and an assortment of Bells of Ireland toppled out the top of sterling silver bowls.

When considering possible options for a favor, I wanted something that was unique, that would support the theme of the event, and that would coordinate with the table design. I had used the bookmark concept for the invitation, so I looked to Diana Laursen, a wonderful young entrepreneur from Waynesville, North Carolina. Diana's business, Hazelwood Soap Company, specializes in custom designs of soaps, lotions, candles, and other delightful indulgences. For this event I chose a lightly scented lavender soy candle, and Diana custom made a simple label reading "Children—The Light of Annette's Life." I chose the color of the ribbon and box to harmonize with the table design, and Diana completed my favor with a personal monogram on the exterior of the box. Oh, how I do love design flexibility and Diana's willingness to create it!

A GRANDMOTHER'S BOOK SHOWER MENU

COCKTAIL
La Vie en Rose

FIRST COURSE
Butternut Squash Soup with
Toasted Pistachios and Local Honey

SECOND COURSE
Mixed Lettuces with Roasted Beets,
Avocado, and Blood Orange Vinaigrette

THIRD COURSE
Maine Lobster with Ricotta Gnocchi
and Lemon Cream

FOURTH COURSE
Vanilla Bean Panna Cotta with Braised Berries

La Vie en Rose Champagne Cocktail

This is a festive cocktail that I first had in Paris.

- ⚜ ½ shot glass rose water
- ⚜ 1 small sugar cube
- ⚜ Rosé Champagne
- ⚜ Raspberries for garnishing

Soak the sugar cube in the rose water and place in a champagne flute. Add Rosé Champagne into the flute until full. If you do not have rose water, you can make your own. Wash rose petals and add them to boiling water. Let cool. Garnish the cocktail with a raspberry.

Butternut Squash Soup with Toasted Pistachios

- ✢ 2 large butternut squash, seeded and cut into large chunks
- ✢ Melted butter for brushing the squash
- ✢ 2 teaspoons sea salt
- ✢ 3 cups chicken stock or low-sodium chicken broth
- ✢ 3 tablespoons local honey, plus some extra for garnishing
- ✢ 4 Granny Smith apples, peeled, seeded, and cut into 2-inch cubes
- ✢ ¾ cup heavy cream
- ✢ ½ teaspoon freshly grated nutmeg
- ✢ ½ teaspoon ginger
- ✢ Salt and pepper to taste
- ✢ Toasted pistachios for garnishing

Preheat oven to 425 degrees. Brush the squash with melted butter and season with sea salt. Roast on a lined baking sheet with the squash flesh side up for 30 minutes or until the squash is soft.

Scoop the squash flesh from the skin and place in a saucepan. Add the chicken stock, honey, and apple cubes. Let simmer until apples are soft. Blend with an immersion blender until smooth. Stir in the heavy cream and let simmer for an additional 15 minutes. Season with the nutmeg, ginger, and salt and pepper to taste. Garnish with a drizzle of honey and toasted pistachios.

When not being used, many of the pieces are showcased in display cabinets in Annette's kitchen and prep kitchen.

As guests arrived, they were given a La Vie en Rose, a rose-scented champagne cocktail, to enjoy as they mingled. This cocktail is sweet, bubbly loveliness in a glass, and it was just the treat to kick off our celebration.

The first course was a warm, rich butternut squash soup, which was perfect for the winter day. A refreshing greens salad with roasted beets and avocado followed. Our main course was Maine lobster with ricotta gnocchi. After opening her gifts of lovely children's books that would be shared for many generations, Annette invited guests to have their dessert of panna cotta and coffee around the fire.

It was a wonderful afternoon celebrating the blessing of a first grandchild with one of my most treasured friends.

MASON'S IRONSTONE STRATHMORE BLUE

The history of this vibrant pattern begins at the start of the nineteenth century. "Ironstone" refers to the pattern's white clay, earthenware base. A much stronger, heavier, and more chip-resistant alternative to porcelain, it quickly became a popular option and was an instant success. Strathmore Blue is a multicolored floral, blue-basket design with hints of rosy pinks, vibrant greens, and warm yellows. It was manufactured in a much smaller quantity in a lovely pink pattern, and today pieces of this pink pattern are rare finds. Mason's Vista is a lovely and compatible pattern to mix with Strathmore Blue.

As Annette and I worked to create her dream kitchen several years ago, Strathmore Blue was a superb fit and a wonderful addition to her already impressive collection of fine china patterns. When not being used for entertaining, many of the pieces hang on exposed brick walls and in display cabinets in Annette's kitchen and prep kitchen. Considering that this event was meant to honor Annette, there was no question that this pattern would be the perfect choice for her Grandmother's Book Shower.

The production of Royal Lace
started in 1934. The blue pattern
was created to avoid wasting a
batch of molten blue glass during
the American Depression.

Grandmother's Shower Luncheon

Cocktail
La Vie en Rose - a rose scented champagne cocktail

First Course
Butternut squash soup with toasted pistachio & local honey

Second Course
Mixed lettuces with roasted beet, avocado
& blood orange vinaigrette

Third Course
Maine lobster with ricotta gnocchi & lemon cream

Fourth Course
Vanilla bean panna cotta with braised berries

HAZELWOOD
SOAP COMPANY

WWW.HAZELWOODSOAPCOMPANY.COM

Winnie

ROYAL LACE DEPRESSION GLASS

On a trip to Replacements, Ltd., I found the beautiful depression glass pattern Royal Lace in cobalt blue. I felt it would be a brilliant accent piece for the Mason's Ironstone pattern, and I was right. It catches the eye and accentuates the blues of the Mason's pattern. I wanted it to play a supporting role in this particular table setting and chose to use only the soup bowl and its under plate. Annette loved the diversity of these pieces and will use them for soups, fruits, and desserts. The simplicity of this pattern makes it the perfect addition to most of Annette's china patterns, all of which have blue in their color palettes.

The production of Royal Lace started in 1934. The blue pattern was created to avoid wasting a batch of molten blue glass when the project it was meant for was suddenly halted due to hard times during the American Depression. Lucky for the Hazel-Atlas Glass Company, this last minute idea resulted in what quickly became its most popular pattern. Today it is one of the most highly sought after and expensive of all Depression glass patterns. Great story for a dinner party, don't you think?

CHAPTER 4

BLACK-TIE BIRTHDAY CELEBRATION

One of my greatest joys is entertaining with my friend Bo Henderson. After a great deal of discussion regarding an upcoming "significant" birthday for his partner, Ed Springs, we decided that an intimate black-tie dinner party for close friends would make a perfect gift. Bo and I have long shared a great passion for collecting china patterns, so we had many collections to choose from. But we both agreed that Flora Danica by Royal Copenhagen was the ultimate china pattern to use in celebrating a major birthday for Ed, the quintessential gentleman and collector.

Bo and Ed have an extensive collection of Flora Danica that they have amassed over several years. This pattern is the pinnacle of floral china and remains in production today, after more than 220 years. The formality of this pattern makes it a treasure, and, despite its value, Bo and Ed are not afraid to use it for special entertaining events. Any revered collection becomes even more special when used to celebrate with friends and family.

Celebrate!

PLEASE JOIN US TO

CELEBRATE

*Ed's
Birthday*

SATURDAY, JULY 10, 2010

SEVEN O'CLOCK IN THE EVENING

GOLDEN HILL

362 WONDERLAND TRAIL

BLACKTIE

THE INVITATION REFLECTED THE GRANDNESS AND FORMALITY OF THE EVENING TO COME.

The aubergine-glazed dining room features an Italian gilded chandelier and is filled with treasured antiques.

Ideally, we would have invited many more of Ed's friend to this black-tie celebration, but the Flora Danica service for twelve required us to keep the party intimate. We had the invitation scripted on off-white linen paper and framed in black and gold card stock, and we included a classic gold ribbon at the top. This invitation reflected the grandness and formality of the evening to come, and it certainly seemed an invitation worthy of the gentleman of honor.

The deep aubergine-glazed dining room of Bo and Ed's mountain home features an Italian gilded chandelier and is filled with treasured antiques. Since they often entertain for groups of twelve, they designed a custom, oval-shaped table that is perfect for intimate dinner parties. Ed's collection of antique portrait plates hangs around the room. The draperies are made of aubergine- and green-checked silk with delicately embroidered flowers. A trumeau mirror hangs over an antique French sideboard that displays additional pieces made by Royal Copenhagen, along with the evening's wine selection. Above the fireplace hangs a copy of a painting depicting Louis XIV by Velasquez. The antique Sevres mantle garniture holds arrangements of Flora Danica–inspired pastel flowers. The room glows with gilding and the soft radiance of sterling silver.

An antique French sideboard displays additional pieces made by Royal Copenhagen, along with the evening's wine selection.

THE FLORA DANICA PATTERN IS THE PINNACLE OF FLORAL CHINA AND REMAINS IN PRODUCTION TODAY, AFTER MORE THAN 220 YEARS.

The star of this tabletop was undoubtedly the Flora Danica collection, and Bo and I designed each element with this in mind. We topped an aubergine undercloth with a delicate gold overlay to create a rich base for the table setting. To ensure that nothing on the table would take away from the grandness of the Flora Danica, we positioned the scripted place cards atop the Palais crystal. This intricate pattern of cut crystal features gold laurels and dots with a gold rim. Sterling silver chargers make a simple statement and emphasize the beauty of this exquisite pattern, which Bayel Crystal discontinued in 1970.

Individual menu cards of metallic gold and linen paper were placed on each napkin. We arranged antique silver pillar candlesticks of varying heights along the center of the oval table to create an avenue of soft, romantic light. A bouquet of pastel flowers arranged in a sterling silver tureen accentuated the delicate color palette of this china collection.

***

As a tribute to the guest of honor, Bo and I designed the menu to feature many of Ed's favorite dishes. We began by serving champagne chilled in an exquisite sterling silver wine cooler and hors d'oeuvres of new potatoes stuffed with caviar and crème fraîche in the living

Located in Bayel, France, the "City of Crystal," Bayel Crystal has been producing fine glassware since the 1660s.

room. This lovely yellow room contains an extensive collection of Blanc de Chine. French for "Chinese White," Blanc de Chine is a traditionally made white-glazed porcelain that was originally introduced by the Chinese and has been reproduced over the years by European and American artisans.

At a leisurely pace, guests moved to the elegant dining room for a meal of carrot soup with boursin whipped cream, a beautiful heirloom tomato caprese salad, followed by Ed's favorite, osso bucco. This dish was served with grilled asparagus and Parmigiano-Reggiano herbed orzo. After a fantastic meal, much reminiscing, and a good deal of French wine, we retired to the library. The intimate atmosphere of this red-glazed room was a perfect end to the evening. We enjoyed coffee and a dessert of peaches with almond crème and almond macaroons, inspired by a *dolce* I enjoyed during a trip to Tuscany. As the evening drew to a close, cummerbunds and high heels came off and we relished the fine evening we shared and toasted to the quintessential gentleman and his extraordinary taste among the lovely collections.

FLORA DANICA

The 1700s were a progressive time in the field of natural sciences. We still use the system for classifying botanicals that was established by Swedish botanist Carl von Linné during that time. In Denmark, after 122 years of study and labor, botanists, adhering to von Linné's classification system, completed a comprehensive publication depicting the wild flora of the kingdom, along with copperplate prints of each plant.

THE PRESTIGE OF FLORA DANICA LIES IN THE DETAILS OF EACH PIECE AND THE UNIQUE RENDERINGS OF THE GLORIOUS FLORA OF THE DANISH COUNTRYSIDE.

BLACK-TIE BIRTHDAY CELEBRATION

New Red Potatoes
Stuffed with Caviar and Crème Fraîche

Carrot Soup with Boursin Whipped Cream

Stacked Heirloom Tomato Caprese Salad

Lemon Sorbet

Osso Bucco with Grilled Asparagus and
Parmigiano-Reggiano Herbed Orzo

Peaches with Almond Crème
and Almond Macaroons

Poached Peaches with Almond Crème

+ 6 large, ripe yellow peaches
+ 1 cup champagne
+ 3 tablespoons sugar
+ 4 cups water

Peel peaches, cut in half, and remove the pit. Bring water, champagne, and sugar to a boil in a saucepan and add 3-4 peach halves at a time. Poach for 5 minutes. Remove the peaches from the liquid and cool completely. Keep the poaching liquid to drizzle on the serving plate after adding the filling. Serves 12.

Almond Crème

+ 8 ounces mascarpone cheese
+ ½ cup crème fraîche
+ ¼ cup heavy cream
+ ¼ cup superfine sugar
+ 2 cups almond cookies, crushed
+ Mint leaves for garnishing
+ ½ cup toasted sliced almonds, plus some extra for garnishing

Mix all ingredients together and chill for 30 minutes. Fill each peach half with the filling mixture. Place on serving plate and garnish with mint leaves and toasted almonds. Drizzle about ⅛ to ¼ cup of the poaching liquid around each peach half.

Note: If crème fraîche is not available, add 1 tablespoon of buttermilk to ½ cup of sour cream.

We served champagne chilled in an exquisite sterling silver wine cooler and hors d'oeuvres of new potatoes stuffed with caviar and crème fraîche in the living room.

The story of Flora Danica, or Danish Flora, began at the end of the eighteenth century when a messenger arrived at the Royal Copenhagen Porcelain Manufactory with a portfolio of botanical illustrations and copper plate prints. Crown Prince Frederik, the future King of Denmark, was inspired by the portfolio to commission the production of a luxurious porcelain dinner service as a gift for the Czarina Catherine II of Russia. The czarina died before production was complete, and it became the dinner service of the royal family of Denmark.

It was essential that the gift be worthy of European Royalty and represent Denmark's natural beauty

and the abilities of its artisans. At the end of twelve years, 1,802 unique pieces of hand-molded, hand-painted porcelain were completed and inaugurated at the royal table of Denmark. This china lived up to its expectations, becoming the most revered china in the world and awing guests lucky enough to see it sparkle in the candlelight of royal occasions. Of the 1,802 original pieces, more than 1,500 remain intact.

Production of Flora Danica ceased for six decades, during which time the emphasis shifted from a comprehensive rendering of the Danish flora to focusing on the aesthetic beauty of select plants. When Princess Alexandra was set to marry the Prince of Wales, and the production of Flora Danica was reinstated, only the most beautiful of Danish flowers were chosen to be hand painted, and in much more vibrant colors than originally rendered. Today, the dinner service created for Alexandra and her king lives at Windsor Palace as part of the collection of the British queen.

The prestige of Flora Danica lies in the details of each piece—individual brushstrokes; every golden pearl; each hand-molded, serrated edge; and the unique renderings of the glorious flora of the Danish countryside. Danish artisans continue to create Flora Danica entirely by hand. After the molding and firing processes are complete, painters sit with a white-glazed porcelain piece and the original copper plates used to inspire the first collection in 1790, and a Danish flora comes alive. In the 220 years of production, no individual piece has ever been replicated. Today, Flora Danica remains the most expensive and celebrated china pattern in the world.

In 220 years of production, no individual piece of Flora Danica has ever been replicated. Today, it remains the most expensive and celebrated china pattern in the world.

CHAPTER 5

BLUE PLATE SPECIAL

A relaxing Sunday evening supper with friends and a meal of comfort foods was the idea behind this Blue Plate Special event. I designed a menu of Southern delights similar to those found on the specials boards at Southern diners, and I featured the divided Blue Willow plates, from which the name Blue Plate Special originated. Our evening consisted of what you might expect: great friends, long conversations, laughter, and full and satisfied tummies.

My dear friend and client, Holli Morris, has a collection of Blue Willow china, both antique and new, that is unparalleled by any other I have seen, and it was this collection that inspired our Blue Plate Special evening. With homes in Waynesville, North Carolina, and Tampa, Florida, Holli splits her collection between both houses. The Blue Willow that she keeps at her mountain house, known to friends and family as "The Chicken Coop," serves beautifully for informal entertaining. Holli combines her Blue Willow with a collection of vintage cobalt glass, and an array of paintings and figurines depicting our feathered friends, for whom her home is named. The Chicken Coop is full of beautiful, informal cottage pieces of old pine and oak, and in this environment the blue willow has a mellow, homey look. Sunday night dinners take on an old diner feel, complete with delicious comfort foods in a casual, easy environment.

The Chicken Coop is full of beautiful, informal cottage pieces of old pine and oak.

The Chicken Coop began life as just that, complete with chicken-feed storage upstairs, and a dog-trot through the middle of the home. The storage area is now a home office, and the dogtrot is now a welcoming, homey foyer. The actual chicken coop was converted into a livable space, and in 1999, Holli and Mike found their ideal summer retreat. Through much cosmetic and structural work they turned it into the comfortable and serene mountain home it is today.

In the open dining area, a compilation of Blue Willow pieces crown the top of a light pine dresser made from reclaimed English wood, and cobalt glass is displayed within its cabinets. On the serving area sits Blue Willow covered dishes, plates, and platters that are easily within reach for everyday use. Walls of painted pine tongue-and-groove paneling offer a fresh, crisp contrast to the Blue Willow. One of the most notable paintings in The Chicken Coop is the John "Cornbread" Anderson piece, "Black Guinea Hens." His abstract interpretations of Georgia farm life are painted on wooden panels and have become widely collected.

The kitchen is hung with Blue Willow, and vintage cobalt pieces sit on almost every surface. Open shelves loaded with Blue Willow, along with some red accents, make cooking and entertaining within arms reach. A long island with a butcher-block top provides a great place for friends to gather and converse while meals are being prepared, and also makes a great place for organizing and serving when entertaining. On one counter sits a lovely Blue Willow needlepoint given to me years ago by a wonderful client that is now on "permanent loan" to Holli. Above the double refrigerators sit antique baskets and more Blue Willow, including a pair of antique vases that Holli and I discovered in a quaint antique shop near Kenmare, Ireland.

Sunday night dinners take on an old diner feel, complete with delicious comfort foods in a casual, easy environment.

A child's table was set up for the children so they could be a part of the evening's festivities.

A compilation of Blue Willow pieces crown the top of a light pine dresser, within reach for everyday use.

Please join Holli and Mike
For a Blue Plate Special Dinner
Featuring our favorite comfort foods
On Sunday evening
March 21
At
6 P.M

Mr. and Mrs. Mark Grantham

I love it when an inexpensive and easy-to-prepare invitation exactly captures the theme of an event.

Considering that it was the china pattern itself that inspired this event, I thought it appropriate to feature it on the invitation. I scanned a brilliant image of a Blue Willow plate, printed it on heavy paper stock, trimmed it, and was delighted with the end result. It was perfectly casual and festive, and it fit the evening's comfortable and easy atmosphere. I love it when an inexpensive and easy-to-prepare invitation exactly captures the theme of an event. I feel like such invitations give my guests a taste of what is in store for them.

Holli's English trestle table, with its dark oak finish, needed no tablecloth, so I used only a combination of casual, everyday blue place mats and blue-and-white checked dinner napkins. The divided grill plates that inspired this Blue Plate Special sat in the center of each setting

The name of each guest was written on small white porcelain place cards that are perfect for casual entertaining.

with casual hotel silverware. Ribbed cobalt tumblers, circa 1930 by Hazel-Atlas Glass Company, sit to the right of each place setting along with some unidentified pilsner glasses. The name of each guest was written on small white porcelain place cards that are perfect for casual entertaining and can be washed clean and used again and again. A combination of unattributed vases from New Martinsville Glass Company, ribbed "Beehive" cobalt vases, circa 1930, held red, yellow, and white tulips, which made a quick and easy centerpiece for this table.

Blue Plate Special
Fried Green Tomatoes
with Pimento Cheese
BLT Wedge Salad
Meat Loaf
Mac & Cheese
Green Beans
Skillet Drop Biscuits
Peach Cobbler
A 'La Modé

BLUE PLATE SPECIAL MENU

Fried Green Tomatoes
with Pimento Cheese

~~~~~

BLT Wedge Salad

~~~~~

Meat Loaf

~~~~~

Miriam's Mac and Cheese

~~~~~

Green Beans

~~~~~

Skillet-Drop Biscuits

~~~~~

Peach Cobbler à la Mode

The development of this menu was undoubtedly inspired by Southern diner foods, and I wrote the evening's food selections on our own special chalkboard, which hung in the kitchen. We began with an appetizer of fried green tomatoes topped with spicy pimento cheese and finished with a balsamic glaze. An old Blue Willow cake stand was perfect for the service of our next course—a bacon, lettuce, and tomato wedge salad topped with a creamy ranch-based dressing. I fell in love with this dressing on a trip to Colorado, while dining at Pinons, one of our favorite restaurants in Aspen. After some unsuccessful cajoling of the maitre d', Wells flashed a twenty dollar bill to the bus boy and I was finally rewarded the recipe for this delicious dressing. There was only one small problem: the ingredient list would make enough dressing for at least fifty people! So, as you might imagine, a little bit of conversion was in order.

For the main course I served meatloaf, macaroni and cheese, green beans, and skillet-drop biscuits. With this menu, I'm sharing with you a recipe close to my heart—my late mother-in-law Miriam Greeley's own version of mac and cheese, which includes creamy cottage cheese and is a unique take on traditional mac and cheese recipes.

For the thirty years that I have attended the Furniture Market in High Point, North Carolina, I have been lucky to stay with my long-time friend, Kathy Tabor West. Together, we pour over cookbooks in the evenings after long, hard days at the market. During each of my visits, I am treated to homemade skillet-drop biscuits, cooked in one of Kathy's well-seasoned, cast-iron frying pans. She gladly shared her recipe, which was handed down through her mother's family for many generations.

Homemade peach cobbler à la mode was served in footed, vintage cobalt sherbet bowls with new, Willow-patterned napkins and was enjoyed around a toasty fire.

Chestnut Cottage is steeped in English and Irish designs, and we have always enjoyed English parlor games. Several years ago, Holli had given me a delightful parlor game based on the Willow legend. After a bit of online research, I was able to find this same parlor game, which we gave out as a party favor. After sharing our meal of comfort foods, those who were still awake gathered in front of a crackling fire, sipped after-dinner drinks, and played the Blue Willow parlor game.

The evening was wonderfully comfortable, with lots of delicious Southern foods, laughter, and old friends coming together for a relaxing dinner. It was just what Holli and I had hoped for. We had turned Holli and Mike's home into a homecookin' country diner for the night, and I ask you, what better venue for a blue plate special than The Chicken Coop?

After sharing our meal of comfort foods, those who were still awake gathered in front of a crackling fire, sipped after-dinner drinks, and played the Blue Willow parlor game.

Following is a poem that describes the fable associated with the Blue Willow pattern:

Whilst we sit around the table,
Please allow me to relate,
The entrancing ancient fable
Of "The Willow Pattern Plate."

Every picture tells a story,
Like the Willow Pattern Plate,
Where two lovers dwelt in glory,
And defied paternal hate.

By elopement from the castle
You observe upon the ridge,
Where the violent old rascal
Chases them across the bridge.

Tries to catch the rogue and whip him,
'Ere he steals the daughter fair;
But the loving pair outstrip him,
Let him languish in despair.

Thrown upon their own resources,
In a junk they emigrate,
To a splendid little oasis,
Near the margin of the plate.

Dwell in peace, whilst unmolested,
In most perfect harmony;
Till at length they are arrested,
by his Nib's gendarmerie.

Then the tyrant lord appeals to
Law and lucre, with their pow'r;
Caught, confined, they have
their meals too,
In that horrid little tow'r.

When the pair are executed,
To appease their lord irate,
To a pair of doves transmuted,
Still they fly upon the plate.

Every picture tells a story,
Like the Willow Pattern blue,
And true love will reign in glory,
To infinity! Adieu

— B. L. BOWERS

A STORY UNFOLDS
ON EACH PIECE
OF BLUE WILLOW
CHINA: FORBIDDEN
LOVE, HOPE, A
JOURNEY, A TRAGEDY,
AND A BLESSING
FROM THE GODS.

BLUE WILLOW

A story unfolds on each piece of Blue Willow china: forbidden love, hope, a journey, a tragedy, and a blessing from the gods play out under the willow trees of this earthenware pattern. The pattern tells a pictorial story of a Chinese legend in elaborate and intricate designs. Part of the fascination of the Willow pattern is the speculation and uncertainty over the actual story, but most agree that it is the tale of two lovers destined to be together, even through death. The story of Koong-se and her Chang is simply and beautifully shared through words and incredible drawings in a lovely picture book, *The Willow Pattern Story*, by Lucienne Fontannaz.

Blue Willow is said to be the most collected china pattern ever made.

The English pattern was first created by Spode in 1790, as an interpretation of an earlier Chinese pattern and fable, but over time almost every English potter, Milton (which later merged with Royal Doulton), and Royal Worcester, among others, created their own interpretation of the legend of Blue Willow. New pieces are still being produced, and today's collections of Blue Willow feature pieces from a variety of sources, styles, and time periods, making any collection of the pattern mysterious and exciting. It is said to be the most collected china pattern ever made. The earliest versions of the pattern are often purchased for thousands of dollars by dedicated collectors, happy to pay for a true original.

TODAY'S BLUE WILLOW
COLLECTIONS FEATURE
PIECES FROM A VARIETY
OF SOURCES, STYLES,

AND TIME PERIODS, MAKING
ANY COLLECTION OF THE
PATTERN MYSTERIOUS
AND EXCITING.

VINTAGE COBALT GLASS

Cobalt glass was first produced during the Depression era, from the 1930s into the early 1940s. Pioneers of this spectacular glass are the Hazel-Atlas Glass Company and Fenton Art Glass Company, and their patterns have been heavily reproduced ever since. During the Depression, wasting any materials was unheard of, and many of these cobalt glass patterns, such as the Royal Lace featured in "A Grandmother's Book Shower," came about as a means of using "leftover" materials.

The deep blue color of this special glass is achieved by incorporating the cobalt oxide element into molten glass. There is truly an art to collecting cobalt glass, and one must be on the lookout for the many reproductions, which are not of the same quality and design of earlier pieces. Although cobalt glass is widely available on the Internet, I recommend sticking with antique stores. As a collector, it is essential to know what you are getting and the history behind the pieces you have discovered. Sifting through reproductions to find the true gems makes the hunt for cobalt glass pieces all the more fun!

Some of Holli's notable pieces of cobalt glass include a butter dish featuring a cow resting on top, and a decanter that, though its maker has never been verified, has been named "ring of rings" by Hazel Marie Weatherman in her 1974 book on colored glassware. It is ten inches high and features a stopper and several three-inch tumblers. One of Holli's favorite pieces is her Hazel-Atlas jug, circa 1939.

As a collector, it is essential to know what you are getting and the history behind the pieces you have discovered.

Miriam's Mac and Cheese

This recipe belonged to my mother-in-law, Miriam Greeley, and was given to me before her death.

+ 8-ounce package elbow macaroni
+ 2 cups cottage cheese
+ 8-ounce carton sour cream
+ 1 egg, slightly beaten
+ 2 cups grated, sharp cheddar cheese, plus ½ cup for the top
+ Salt and pepper to taste
+ Paprika for sprinkling on top

Cook macaroni according to directions, drain, rinse, and set aside. Combine the next five ingredients and mix well. Add the cooked macaroni and spoon the mixture into a lightly greased 2-quart casserole dish. Add ½ cup of the grated cheddar on top and sprinkle with paprika. Bake at 350 degrees for 45 minutes. I often double this recipe and bake in a 9-inch × 13-inch casserole.

Skillet-Drop Biscuits

This recipe is from my friend Kathy Tabor West. The recipe has been passed down from Kathy's maternal grandmother and used by the family for many generations.

- ½ cup Crisco
- 4 cups White Lily Unbleached self-rising flour, sifted
- 1¾ cups buttermilk
- ¼ cup water
- 2 tablespoons butter

Cut Crisco into the flour with a pastry blender or by hand until the flour has formed small lumps. Pour buttermilk and half the water into the mixture and mix by hand until the mixture is soft and fluffy. Add the remaining water as needed to achieve this fluffy consistency. Too much water will make the biscuits flat.

In a black cast-iron skillet, melt the butter, taking care not to burn it. Sprinkle the pan with a little flour and drop large spoonfuls of dough into the pan. The dough biscuits should touch each other on their sides and fill up the pan. Bake at 450 degrees for about 20–25 minutes or until golden brown. Turn the biscuits out of the pan and serve immediately.

CHAPTER 6

OLD-HOLLYWOOD MARTINI PARTY

*W*hen Kathryn Greeley Designs completed a redesign of a client's home in Asheville, North Carolina, that had an old-Hollywood glamour feel, we celebrated the occasion with an intimate martini party for six couples. The redesign incorporated the client's antiques and existing furniture and gave the dated interior a new twist with current styles that didn't have the edginess and harshness of much of today's contemporary furnishings.

This event centered around a collection of twelve handblown martini glasses created by glassblower Kenny Pieper. These glasses are exquisite and every one is unique. They were a fitting tribute to our honoree of the evening, Frank Sinatra.

As guests arrived, they quickly found their way through the foyer to a new, contemporary sideboard made by Currin Furniture, where they were offered a martini in Kenny Pieper's inimitable martini glasses. On the sideboard, I arranged calla lilies, several crystal candlesticks by Simon Pearce, and a collection of the designer's glass bowls for the service of my always popular Rosemary Cocktail Nuts.

A red, rose, white, gold, and aqua color palette runs throughout the open entertaining area of this home. There are two main seating areas in the large living room, one in front of a beautiful bay window and the other around a fireplace. The needlepoint rugs in each space were designed by Kathryn Greeley Designs in conjunction with New River Artisans.

"LET ME FIX YOU A MARTINI THAT'S PURE MAGIC. IT MAY NOT MAKE LIFE'S PROBLEMS DISAPPEAR, BUT IT'LL CERTAINLY REDUCE THEIR SIZE."

—FRANK SINATRA & DEAN MARTIN IN THE 1958 FILM *SOME CAME RUNNING*

The Satterwhite family has built New River Artisans, a custom rug company, for two generations in the New River Valley in the mountains of North Carolina and Southwestern Virginia. They are truly innovators in the development of new techniques for custom rugs and a pleasure to work with for any designer.

In the living room, we combined the client's existing antique French chairs and console with new, more contemporary pieces, such as the coffee table and sofa, and a few pieces of contemporary artwork. The dark wood cabinet in the foyer, with a painted aqua interior, displays my client's large collection of glass, such as Steuben, Baccarat, Tiffany, and Waterford.

The dining room is my favorite room in the house. The table was custom made by John Chapline and his team at Full Circle Furniture Company with design input from Kathryn Greeley Designs. It is a traditional-style table featuring an intricate, looped inlay. This exquisite table is combined with chairs that are reproductions of the George III style. Although English in origin, this style was most certainly the work of French designers, as suggested by the soft curve of the back and the detail work in the armrests. These chairs are covered in a heavy tapestry and backed in aqua silk, and the elegant combination of neo-classical elements and rich upholstery resulted in a uniquely beautiful collection.

In these rooms, French antiques combine beautifully with more contemporary pieces.

The large calla lilies in this aqua green bowl create a stunning everyday centerpiece for this dining table.

The traditional look of the table and chairs blends well with the more contemporary chandelier and sconces. One of the main design features of this room is an entire wall of antique mirrored glass. The dining room rug is also by New River Artisans, and is an example of a much simpler design. In the center of the table sits a beautiful aqua-green bowl that acts as the everyday centerpiece for the table. For this event, I placed two-and-a-half dozen large calla lilies in it for an understated, elegant arrangement.

The kitchen features a very large granite-topped island that is ideal for food preparation or family breakfasts. I adore the client's colorful art-glass roosters next to the stove. The contrast of the painted aqua walls with the bright white of the transitional heavy moldings give this room bold, clean lines.

I commissioned twelve red and gold martini glasses for this event and was blown away by the final product.

Above the client's kitchen desk we displayed this very special collection of martini glasses, a perfect example of my design philosophy—collected, not decorated. No two of the twelve glasses are alike, and the talent and time required to create such beauties demand a prominent display in the home. How depressing to imagine these behind a cabinet door!

The library of this residence is paneled in very distinct butternut wood and features another lovely rug from New River Artisans. The contemporary desk sits in a comfortable niche, and two transitional wing chairs provide a quiet place to read in front of the fire. What a lovely library for one to enjoy while addressing invitations!

I chose a pearlized card stock with a large, loopy font and an image of a martini and then attached it to a red card, creating a small red border. Each rectangular, fourfold envelope, made of heavy stock gold paper, was finished with a golden wax seal. We chose the date of May 14 to honor the death of Frank Sinatra.

attire
ocktail

MARTINI PARTY MENU

Rosemary Cocktail Nuts

Hot Artichoke Dip

Ham Pastry Puffs

Olive Spread Napoleons

Endive Boats with Tuna Tartar and Avocado

Individual Shrimp Cocktails

Chocolate Cups with Lime
Mousse and Raspberries

Ham Pastry Puffs

This recipe came to Chestnut Cottage from one of my husband's employees and has been enjoyed with cocktails for many years.

- ✢ ¼ pound honey baked ham, chopped fine
- ✢ ¼ pound Swiss cheese
- ✢ 1 egg, slightly beaten
- ✢ 8 ounces cream cheese, softened
- ✢ 1 teaspoon red pepper flakes
- ✢ 1 tablespoon fresh chives
- ✢ 1 package of Pepperidge Farm Pastry Puff Sheets

Mix all of the above filling ingredients. Cut puff pastry into twenty-four 2-inch squares. Press squares into ungreased mini-muffin pan. Place a spoonful of filling into each pastry cup. Bake at 400 degrees for 12–15 minutes until slightly browned. Serve hot.

Individual shrimp cocktails were served in mini martini glasses, which are perfect for serving a variety of hors d'oeuvres and desserts. My mother has been making a delicious olive spread as long as I can remember, and, much like the design philosophy of this home, I put a new twist on something old. I layered olive spread between two pecans, and turned it into a bite-sized napoleon hors d'oeuvre. Guest were also treated to my ever popular ham pastry puffs and artichoke dip. Both the artichoke dip and the ham puffs can be assembled ahead of time, and doing so makes for much less last-minute party prep. For a simple dessert I filled chocolate cups with a light lime mouse and added a chocolate and fresh raspberry garnish.

Like the design philosophy of this home, the menu had a new twist on something old.

The evening awash in Hollywood's old glamour was a success, and the night ended with a toast to Mr. Sinatra. To keep the memory of the evening alive, we sent each guest home with CDs of *Ol' Blue Eyes Is Back* and a Rat Pack album, wrapped in pearlized envelopes.

The late afternoon light coming through a dirty martini in this golden glass highlights the distinctiveness and beauty of these glasses.

No two of the twelve glasses are alike. Like the guests at this celebration, this group of individuals make a harmonious and joyful collection.

Using a technique called caneworking, a glass artist uses heat to combine small rods of colored glass and then encases them in clear molten glass that is then molded to the desired shape.

Some martini glasses feature red or gold canes, and others are made with a blend of both colored rods, all creating intricate geometric designs within the glass.

MARTINI GLASSES

Kenny Pieper is an internationally recognized and exhibited glassblower. He has been perfecting his craft since his days as a teenager studying at Penland School of Crafts here in the Blue Ridge Mountains. Continued education and experience in his craft took him to Detroit and the San Francisco Bay Area. In recent years, he has returned to the mountains of North Carolina and produces an incredible body of blown glass vessels and sculptures in his studio in Burnsville, North Carolina.

I commissioned twelve red and gold martini glasses for this event and was blown away by the final product. The details within each glass are intricate and minute, and, as a designer, I enjoyed studying each of them for their subtle and not so subtle differences.

Using a technique called caneworking, a glass artist uses heat to combine small rods of colored glass and then encases them

in clear molten glass that is then molded to the artist's desired shape. Several of the martini glasses Kenny created for me feature one color of canes in red or gold, and others are made with a blending of both colored rods, all creating intricate geometric designs within the glass. Even the stem of each vessel is unique; several sit on four delicate columns of glass, some feature an open circle in the stem design, and still others glow with a spherical ball of color at their bases.

Guests, as I had hoped, were awed by the glass art as well as the cocktail napkins, upon which I had embroidered the message "Cheers."

Hot Artichoke Dip

I have seen many artichoke dips in my years of entertaining, but never one that I like as much as this recipe. A friend gave this to me years ago, and I have slightly changed some of the ingredient amounts to perfect it.

- 4-ounce jar diced pimientos, drained well
- One 14-ounce can artichoke hearts
- Two 7-ounce cans of diced green chilies, drained
- 1 cup Hellmann's mayonnaise
- 4 ounces grated Monterey Jack cheese
- ½ cup grated Parmesan cheese

Mix all of the above ingredients in a mixing bowl. Spoon into a shallow baking dish. Bake uncovered in a preheated 350-degree oven for 30 minutes or until bubbly. Serve with tortilla chips or on crackers.

CHAPTER 7

SCOTTISH GAMEKEEPER'S DINNER

Several years ago, my husband and I traveled to the Scottish Highlands with three other couples for a golf, gourmet, and antiquing adventure. We so enjoyed our time there that we wanted to reunite the couples for an evening to plan a reunion trip. Wells and I hosted a dinner party for our travel companions at our lake house, which was the perfect venue with its Scottish feel and design elements. The menu featured both foods and beverages that we enjoyed in Scotland during our first trip and those that one might experience in the lovely country homes of the Highlands. My collection of "game china" was the main feature for this event.

I invited our guests with a simple ivory folded card with chocolate-brown text and detailing. The pheasant depiction on the front tied in nicely with pheasant place card holders I used on the dining table the evening of our dinner party. The menu card mimicked the invitation's chocolate on ivory, and featured a sketched fox overlooking the evening's delicacies.

Please come for a
"Scottish Gamekeeper's Dinner"
to plan our trip back to the Highlands

Saturday, October 2nd at Lake Chatuge

Single malts and starters at 6:30pm

THE INVITE TIED IN NICELY WITH THE PHEASANT PLACE CARD HOLDERS USED ON THE DINING TABLE.

Scottish design elements are present throughout our lake home and are especially prominent in the living, dining, and kitchen areas.

Scottish design elements are present throughout our lake home and are especially prominent in the living, dining, and kitchen areas. Muted browns, greens, burgundies, and butterscotch tones are punched up within vivid tartans and paisleys, and combined with velvets, florals, tweeds, and Persian carpets. By evening firelight, pale parchment walls add an element of lightness to the living room. Throughout our home, there are a variety of English, Irish, and Scottish antiques. The massive antique table, circa 1820, is English oak with heavy, twisted legs, and is flanked with two antique leather winged chairs and antique Italian side chairs.

The walls of London's Dorchester Hotel are illustrated by artist Mark Beard and depict heroic Highlanders. I commissioned a local artist to paint a similar scene to hang on the stone fireplace in our lake house living room.

One of my favorite spots in London is the newly refreshed and updated Grill at The Dorchester Hotel. The walls of the Grill are illustrated by artist Mark Beard and depict tremendous and heroic Highlanders. These paintings inspired me to commission a local artist to paint a similar scene, which now hangs on the stone fireplace in our lake house living room.

Dinner was served in the open dining room. The table setting began with a wool plaid tablecloth and wool houndstooth napkins. The napkin rings are English, circa the early 1900s, and are a beautiful polished wood banded in silver. An old wooden charger held the

various game china patterns, and I chose an antique sterling and stag antler cutlery by George Butler and Co., of Sheffield, England. This company has been producing the finest-quality cutlery since the late 1600s. I mixed the beautiful Thistle crystal pattern with my Waterford Curraghmore. A treen trophy bowl filled with leonidas roses, hypericum, and pittosporum sat in the center of the table surrounded by barley twist candlesticks. An old pine breadboard held a warm round loaf of delicious, crusty bread.

I featured a variety of foods that might be found on a gamekeeper's table at a classic Highland dinner party. Scottish salmon and foie gras seemed a natural choice to accompany single malt whisky cocktails by the fire. Wells and I have fond memories of a rich and creamy mushroom, leek, and potato soup we enjoyed in the Highlands, so I recreated it for our guests with the recipe generously passed on by the owners of the restaurant.

On a trip to New York City many years ago, I was served roasted Scottish pheasants with apricot and dates at the 21 Club. I delighted in the delicacy and was pleased to come across a similar recipe years later in *Bon Appetit*. I was thrilled when our guests enjoyed it just as much as I had. We finished the meal with a warm gooey bread pudding topped with a caramel-whisky sauce.

I mixed the beautiful Thistle crystal pattern with my Waterford Curraghmore.

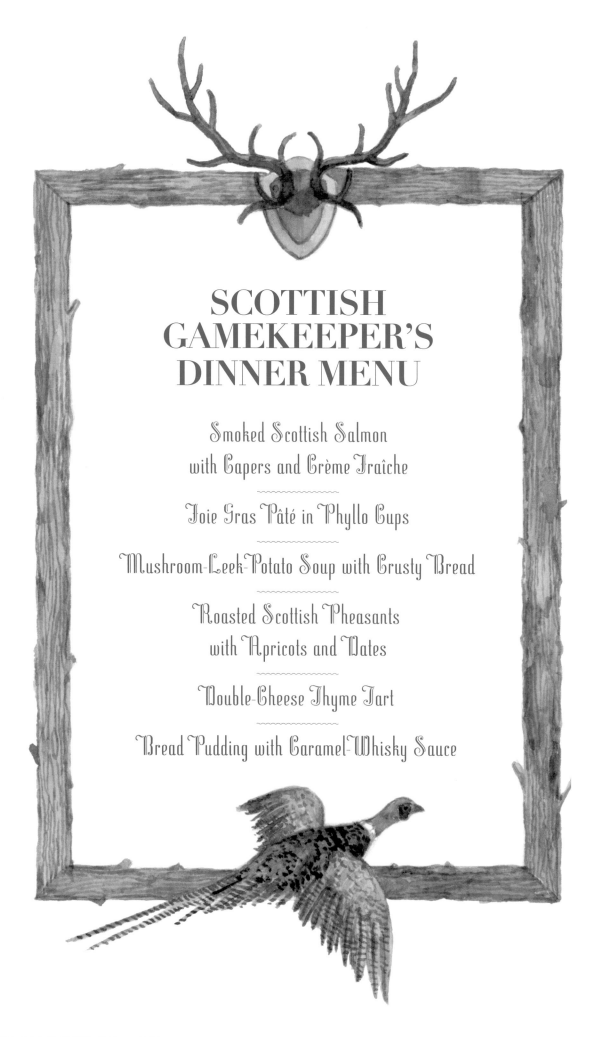

SCOTTISH GAMEKEEPER'S DINNER MENU

Smoked Scottish Salmon
with Capers and Crème Fraîche

Foie Gras Pâté in Phyllo Cups

Mushroom-Leek-Potato Soup with Crusty Bread

Roasted Scottish Pheasants
with Apricots and Dates

Double-Cheese Thyme Tart

Bread Pudding with Caramel-Whisky Sauce

Menu

Smoked Scottish Salmon with Capers and Crème Fraîche
Foie Gras Pâté in Filo Cups

Mushroom-Leek-Potato Soup with Crusty Bread

Roasted Scottish Pheasants with Apricots and Dates
"21" Club and Rabbit Cheese Elixir Tart

Bread Pudding with Caramel-Whiskey Sauce

Wells

WE SENT EACH COUPLE HOME WITH A HAND-NUMBERED BOTTLE OF AN EXCEPTIONAL SINGLE MALT.

As the evening wound down, we sipped Balvenie fifteen-year-old single malt whisky by the fire. Each bottle of this Scottish spirit is unique, inimitable, and one of approximately 350 bottles from a particular cask of whisky. We sent each couple home with a hand-numbered bottle of this exceptional single malt as a memento of our fine Scottish Gamekeeper evening and the adventure to come!

GAME CHINA

My game china collection includes four distinct patterns, and I chose three to use for this event. Czechoslovakian manufacturer Bernadotte's lovely game china depicts animals such as foxes, boars, and stags in their natural settings. This white pattern maintains a delicate look with beautifully embossed rims trimmed in gold.

Johnson Brothers Game Birds pattern, manufactured between 1953–1976, features hunted birds like pheasants, ruffed grouse, quail, and partridge. The bird illustration dominates each piece, and with simple, rounded edges and a white background, this pattern is strong and unpretentious.

Spode's Woodlands pattern was first manufactured in 1991 and is still in production. It features a variety of game, birds, and fish, and each illustration is surrounded by a brown floral design reminiscent of those popular in early nineteenth-century England. Spode adds to the pattern each year and has recently released pieces featuring hunting dog depictions.

Mushroom-Leek-Potato Soup

I had a similar soup on a trip to Scotland and have since reinvented it.

- ⊹ 2 tablespoons unsalted butter
- ⊹ 3 medium leeks, white part only
- ⊹ ½ teaspoon minced garlic
- ⊹ 2 large russet potatoes, peeled and cubed to ¼ inch
- ⊹ 4 cups chicken stock
- ⊹ About 15 baby portobello mushrooms, sliced
- ⊹ 1 cup heavy cream
- ⊹ Salt and pepper to taste
- ⊹ 3 tablespoons sherry
- ⊹ Fried leeks or chives for garnishing

Melt butter in a large stockpot. Cook the leeks and garlic until only slightly browned. Add the cubed potatoes, chicken stock, and mushrooms. Simmer until the potatoes are tender. Remove one half of this mixture from stockpot and set aside. Blend remaining ingredients with an immersion blender until smooth. Return remaining mixture to stockpot and add the cream and salt and pepper to taste. Add the sherry and garnish with fried leeks or chives.

CRYSTAL COLLECTION

Recently I discovered a crystal pattern that left me speechless. On one of my visits, my friend Sandra Jones at Replacements Ltd., knowing that I appreciate fine crystal and that it would mix beautifully with one of my favorite Waterford patterns, Curraghmore, excitedly unveiled Thistle by Edinburgh Crystal Company. The highly distinctive thistle shapes are embellished with a complex geometric pattern and delicate engravings. This classic design, which has remained largely unchanged for more than a century, displays the exceptional skill and quality for which Edinburgh Crystal is renowned. The Edinburgh Crystal Company was founded in 1867 and remains at the cutting edge of contemporary crystal design. They combine a rich historical heritage with a modern outlook and employ the latest in design and manufacturing techniques with traditional skill and values. The talented craftsmen and passionate design team at Edinburgh Crystal are passionate about these exquisite pieces. The Thistle pattern was made in a variety of pieces, including wine, champagne, brandy, and whisky glasses, and wine and whisky decanters.

TREENWARE

"Treen" refers to small wooden objects used in daily living. To be considered treen, a wooden object must serve a purpose rather than being simply ornamental. The list of possible treenware is endless: candlesticks, water pitchers, bowls, nutcrackers, and trays for the home. Hardwoods such as birch, poplar, butternut, oak, and wild cherry were most often used for carving these pieces because of the sturdiness and longevity they offered. In the early 1500s, industries developed alternatives to treenware, and glass, tin, and other metals began to replace these wooden implements. Despite this, treen has survived through the ages and is now quite collectible. Through the years, I have collected a large number of barley twist candlesticks, wooden bowls, and wooden jugs, all of which are considered treenware. The treen pitcher used for this dinner party is made of oak with a silverplate banding, circa the late 1800s. It is called a "Bacchus Jug," referring to Bacchus, the Roman God of wine, who is depicted on the spout.

An antique Scottish chair sits at the kitchen desk and easily converts to a stepladder for moving collections.

Individual Bread Pudding with Caramel-Whisky Sauce

I learned to make this bread pudding at the Cooking School of Aspen, and I added the caramel-whisky sauce by adjusting a caramel cake icing recipe. Sometimes I use croissants as the bread for a softer texture. Makes 8–10 servings in 4-inch ramekins.

- ✦ 1 untrimmed loaf of day-old French bread, or day-old croissants cut into 1-inch cubes
- ✦ ¼ cup unsalted butter, melted
- ✦ 6 eggs, beaten
- ✦ 1½ cups sugar
- ✦ 5 cups milk
- ✦ 2 tablespoons pure vanilla extract
- ✦ ½ teaspoon fresh, grated nutmeg

Preheat oven to 350 degrees. Butter eight individual 4-inch ramekins. Fill ramekins ¾ full with bread cubes and brush with melted butter. In a large bowl, beat eggs and sugar until smooth. Pour milk in while stirring, and add vanilla. Strain this mixture and pour over the bread cubes until the ramekins are full. Place the ramekins in a large roasting pan and surround with hot water. Bake at 350 degrees for 45 minutes, or until set and golden. Remove to a cooling rack and top each ramekin with caramel-whisky sauce.

Caramel-Whisky Sauce

+ 1 stick unsalted butter
+ 2 cups light brown sugar
+ ¼ teaspoon salt
+ ½ cup evaporated milk
+ 1 teaspoon pure vanilla extract
+ ¼ cup single malt Scotch whisky

In a saucepan, combine butter, brown sugar, and salt. Cook over low heat until the sugar dissolves. Add the evaporated milk and cook at a low boil for 3 minutes. Remove from heat, let cool for a few minutes, and add whisky and vanilla. Pour over the individual bread puddings.

Wells

CHAPTER 8

A WEE IRISH SURPRISE

When my husband and I first visited Ireland, I fell in love with both the island itself and the roots I discovered as I explored the home of my ancestors. It had been one of my greatest desires to visit the country my grandfather lived in before immigrating to the United States around 1900. Situated in the hills of County Down in Northern Ireland, Ballycastle House holds a part of my family's history and a piece of my heart. This charming Irish home, formerly a part of the world-renowned Mount Stewart Estate, is situated in the middle of the Ards Peninsula on the sheltered east coast of Ireland. It is now a lovely bed-and-breakfast owned by Margaret and Ronnie Deering.

During our first trip, Wells wished many times for his golfing buddies and eighteen holes at the Royal Downs Golf Club, a majestic golf course just down the road from Ballycastle House. For his fiftieth birthday gift, I planned to make that wish come true.

Menu

Cocktails in the Garden
Shelbourne Mushrooms-Irish Whiskey

First Course
Pickled Beet and Goat Cheese Salad
Lemon Verbena Sorbet

Main Course
Baked Red Trout Encrusted in Pistachios
Green Bean Bundles
Traditional Ulster Champ
Rosemary and Cheddar Scones

Dessert
Irish Golf Course Cake
Cheese Tray with Irish Biscuits and Port

"LONG AGO, WHEN
MEN CURSED AND BEAT
THE GROUND WITH
STICKS, IT WAS CALLED
WITCHCRAFT. TODAY
IT IS CALLED GOLF."

—IRISH SAYING

The invitation featured a small watercolor of Ballycastle House.

Enlisting the help of our great friend, Mike Morris, I secretly planned a two-week adventure for my wonderful husband and six of our close friends. Mike helped choose the golf courses to be played, and I focused on the hotel and restaurant selections and activities for the ladies in attendance. When the trip was planned and the date drew closer, it was time for A Wee Irish Surprise dinner party, during which the surprise would be unveiled.

I introduced the Irish-themed evening by selecting an invitation with a border of gold-and-green plaid, and then scanned a small watercolor of Ballycastle House that had been painted by my dear friend Ed Springs.

The day of the party came, and Wells left to play a round of golf at the local country club with three golfing buddies, who would actually be his companions on our upcoming trip. I peered over my teacup as he gave me a goodbye kiss on my cheek and, upon hearing the tires roll down the hill, jumped to my feet, overjoyed that the day had finally come to reveal his gift. There was much work to be done at Chestnut Cottage in the few hours before A Wee Irish Surprise!

My English-style cottage garden is truly a labor of love and nothing pleases me more than to share it with friends. This May evening, we had cocktails among peonies, roses, and lilacs in full bloom. I served cocktails and hors d'oeuvres in an area of the Chestnut

Cottage gardens that features an old, outdoor fireplace. I built a small fire that evening to tamper the cool mountain air we so often experience on spring and summer evenings in western North Carolina.

On a teak table in the garden, I arranged flowers in one of my beloved Irish sterling plate rings made by Hamilton & Inches of Edinburgh, Scotland, in the late 1800s. These dish rings can be used to hold flower arrangements simply by setting a plastic container inside of the ring. I served Irish Whiskey alongside stuffed mushrooms that were inspired by a recipe I begged for at the

I served Irish Whiskey alongside stuffed mushrooms inspired by a recipe from the Shelbourne Hotel in Dublin.

Shelbourne Hotel in Dublin. This hotel sits across the street from Saint Stephen's Green, the largest park in Dublin's Georgian Squares. For a fantastic read about the history of the Shelbourne Hotel, I recommend *The Shelbourne Hotel* by Elizabeth Bowen.

For a traditional Irish pub feel during cocktails, I chose music by Irish-born Van Morrison and played my all-time favorite song, "Brown Eyed Girl." *Irish Heartbeat*, Van Morrison and the Chieftains' eighteenth album, features the incomparable sounds of the Irish fiddle and exudes intoxicating energy. I played it to create an upbeat mood to start the evening.

Our Irish meal was served in the gathering room of Chestnut Cottage. Inspired by my travels to the British Isles, the room is finished with tone-on-tone green English wallpaper and many great finds I have collected during my antiquing trips in England, Scotland, and Ireland. During dinner I calmed the mood with the peaceful, celtic sounds of the Irish-Norwegian duo Secret Garden. It was a wonderful setting for our meal of Irish delights.

The incomparable sounds of the Irish fiddle exude an intoxicating energy and create an upbeat mood.

The oak Welsh Dresser that showcases my Napolean Ivy collection was one of my first antique pieces.

During my first visit to Ireland, I was amazed at how truly green the Emerald Isle actually is. With the eye of an interior designer, I was struck by the endless shades of green in the Irish landscape. I found harmony and peace in this monochromatic mosaic, and I reached back to those moments of awe for inspiration as I designed the tabletop for Wells's Irish birthday celebration.

BLESS THIS HOUSE

Bless this house O Lord we pray.

Keep it safe by night and day.

Bless these walls so firm and stout,

Keeping want and trouble out.

Bless the roof and chimney tall,

Let thy peace lie over all.

Bless the doors that they may prove

Ever open to joy and love.

Bless the windows shining bright,

Letting in God's heavenly light.

Bless the hearth a-blazing there,

with smoke ascending like a prayer.

Bless the people here within . . .

Keep them pure and free from sin.

Bless us all that one day we

May be fit, O Lord, to dwell with thee.

—AN IRISH BLESSING FOR THE HOME

I love to stockpile great finds like these antique silver place card holders for future events.

I began with a simple white linen tablecloth. I selected a charger plate by Anna Weatherley in a mossy green shade with a gilded, scalloped edge. I found that when I placed the Napoleon Ivy atop this charger it created an aesthetically pleasing, monochromatic contrast that was reminiscent of the Irish landscape—and managed to spotlight the subtle Wedgewood pattern.

On an antiquing trip to West Palm Beach, Florida, I literally wandered into Devonia Antiques, specialists in antiques for dining, and was fortunate to find continental champagne/sherbet glasses made by Val St. Lambert, circa 1920, which I used for sorbet service between courses. These intricate glasses are green cased with gilded cameo figures on an acid-etched background. They are truly unique and added a touch of formality to my place settings.

My antique silver place card holders, monogrammed simply with a *G*, held fantastic, golf-themed place cards that I found at Il Papiro, a delightful paper shop I frequent when in New York City. I love to collect and stockpile great finds like these for future events.

If there is an event more appropriate for using my Waterford crystal pattern, Lismore, made in Ireland since the late 1700s, I cannot imagine what it would be. I used the water glass, balloon wine glass, and the toasting flute, as well as a variety of candlesticks for continuity on the table.

If there is an event more appropriate for using my Waterford crystal pattern, I cannot imagine what it would be.

With a rather formal tabletop, I couldn't resist adding a whimsical element—a glass trumpet vase filled with golf balls and white tees. I topped the vase with mounds of Bells of Ireland, white tulips and roses, snapdragons, lisianthus, stock, and Casablanca lilies. This arrangement was the perfect finishing touch on the table and served as a wonderful expression of the golf-themed trip to come.

For a less formal golf-inspired meal, consider using a similar centerpiece with rustic twig place mats, white napkins tied with real ivy, and individual ivy topiaries with place cards held in place by a golf ball glued to a tee.

The intimacy of this event allowed me do something extra special for the favors. I knew instantly that I would use the event as a way to share some highlights of the upcoming trip.

For the men joining Wells on his tour of four Irish golf courses, I selected a beautiful book by John Redmond, *Great Golf Courses of Ireland*. Within its pages were brilliant pictures taken of the lush, rolling courses that Ireland is so famous for. Several of the courses they would be playing were featured in this wonderful gift that would entice their imaginations leading up to the trip and serve as a reminder of an adventure with friends long after the trip had ended.

For a less formal golf-inspired meal, consider using a similar centerpiece with rustic twig place mats and individual ivy topiaries.

Four ladies left to their own devices in Ireland . . . what to do? I planned a visit to the Ballymaloe Cooking School in County Cork. Local ethnic cooking styles and recipes fascinate me, and I have visited a variety of culinary schools throughout my travels. My favor to the ladies was a cookbook created by Darina Allen, owner of the Ballymaloe Cooking School. I also incorporated a variation of Darina's scone recipe into my menu.

The most special favor of this event was the antique sterling silver trophy that I planned to reveal to Wells during cocktail hour. I have long believed that memories and experiences make amazing gifts. This trophy was the tangible symbol of the adventure I had planned for Wells. The garden provided the perfect setting for presenting the trophy, testament of the journey to come, and, more immediately, a fine Irish meal. My rather modest husband was at first hesitant to open his gift in front of our guests. After a bit of persuasion he agreed, and the look of shock that came over his face was just what I had hoped for.

The most special gift of this event was the antique sterling silver trophy that I had specially inscribed.

For the sake of remembrance, I inscribed the following:

The Wells Greeley Fiftieth Birthday Ireland Foursome
August 2002
Wells Greeley
Ron Leatherwood
Mike Morris
John Shug
Royal County Down, Royal Portrush,
Ballybunion, Waterville

I HAVE LONG BELIEVED THAT MEMORIES AND EXPERIENCES MAKE THE MOST AMAZING GIFTS.

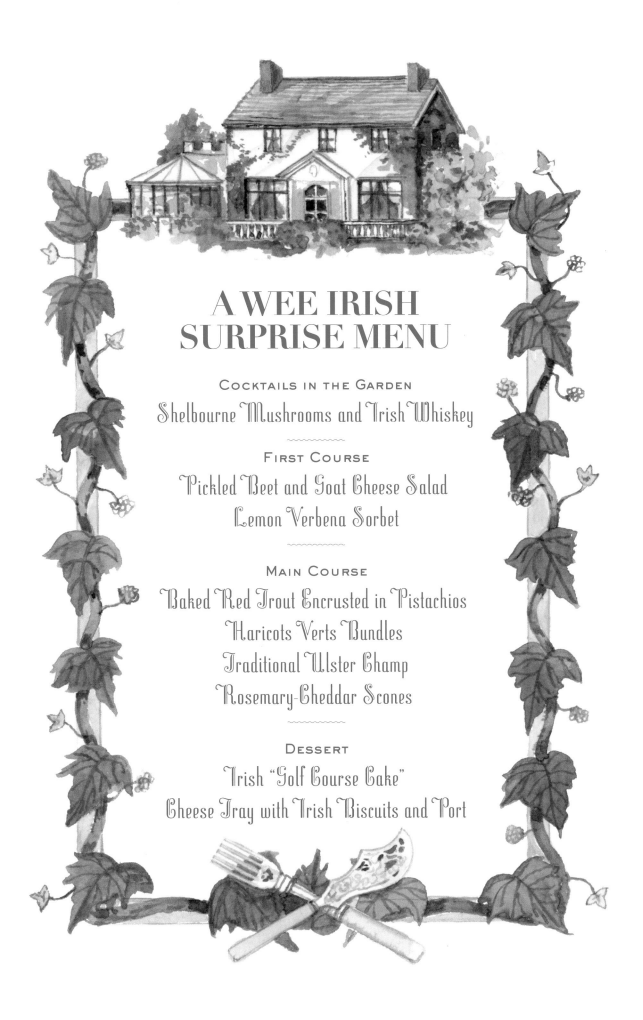

A WEE IRISH SURPRISE MENU

COCKTAILS IN THE GARDEN
Shelbourne Mushrooms and Irish Whiskey

FIRST COURSE
Pickled Beet and Goat Cheese Salad
Lemon Verbena Sorbet

MAIN COURSE
Baked Red Trout Encrusted in Pistachios
Haricots Verts Bundles
Traditional Ulster Champ
Rosemary-Cheddar Scones

DESSERT
Irish "Golf Course Cake"
Cheese Tray with Irish Biscuits and Port

The menu for the evening needed to reflect the Irish theme of the event and offer guests a glimpse into the delicacies they could expect during our upcoming trip. I planned a very special feast with fresh, local ingredients. I cannot say enough about the importance of fresh ingredients in preparing a fine meal. Oftentimes the best dishes have only a few ingredients, allowing the whole foods to speak for themselves, and these dishes will be only as delicious as the ingredients are fresh and of high quality. For this reason I look first to my local farmers. The goat cheese for the pickled beet salad came from Dark Cove Farm, a wonderful goat farm in Cullowhee, North Carolina. The beets came from a wonderful client of mine who home-cans pickled beets for friends each fall. For the main dish I picked up red trout from our friends Sally and Steve Easton, owners of Sunburst Trout Farm, the morning of the event. It was a quick trip to the farm, which is just

After dessert, we stepped next door to a neighbor's guest cabin for cheese, Irish biscuits, and port.

Pickled Beet and Goat Cheese Salad with Walnut Oil Vinaigrette

Each fall a wonderful client gives me several jars of her home-canned pickled beets, which I use in this tasty salad.

‡ Assorted baby greens (often I use baby spinach instead)
‡ ¾ cup walnuts, lightly toasted
‡ 5-7 slices of pickled beets
‡ Goat cheese rounds

To assemble the salad, toss the baby greens with the walnut oil vinaigrette. Place greens on a salad plate and place one or two goat cheese rounds in the center of the greens. Surround the rounds with slices of pickled beets. Garnish with toasted walnuts. Drizzle with additional vinaigrette if desired.

Goat Cheese Rounds

- ✢ 8 ounces soft fresh goat cheese
- ✢ 1 cup Panko (Japanese bread crumbs)
- ✢ 2 teaspoons chopped fresh parsley
- ✢ 2 teaspoons chopped fresh tarragon
- ✢ 1 egg, beaten

Shape the goat cheese into desired size rounds. Combine the panko and the herbs. Brush each ball with the beaten egg and then roll in the crumb mixture until coated, pressing the crumbs into the cheese. Flatten each ball into a disk. Place the disks on a parchment-lined baking sheet and place in the freezer for 20 minutes. Remove from freezer and bake at 425 degrees for 5–6 minutes until lightly browned.

Walnut Oil Vinaigrette

- ✢ 2 teaspoons Dijon mustard
- ✢ 3 tablespoons sherry vinegar
- ✢ 3 tablespoons white wine vinegar
- ✢ ¾ teaspoon sea salt
- ✢ ½ teaspoon black pepper
- ✢ 2 tablespoons honey
- ✢ ½ cup vegetable oil
- ✢ ¼ cup walnut oil

Whisk together all ingredients except the oils, then slowly whisk in the oils in a slow stream. Set aside to allow flavors to blend.

For dessert, I baked a pound cake, my husband's favorite, in the shape of Ireland.

down the road from Chestnut Cottage, nestled in the shadows of the Pisgah National Forest. In three generations, this unique gourmet resource has expanded to offer not only the red trout fillets that I use so often when entertaining, but also cold smoked trout, a great trout dip, and three trout caviars. The highest-quality ingredients make the meal, and the extra planning and effort required to find these items are more than worth the trouble when your guests savor every last bite.

The baked red trout encrusted in pistachios is awe-inspiring when displayed on a plate all by itself, so I chose to include only a few side items. I blanched green beans, tied them into a bundle with a lean strip of bacon, and lightly brushed them with a butter and brown sugar mixture. And of course, no Irish meal is complete without traditional ulster champ, better known to those of us in the States as mashed potatoes. I don't eat many mashed potatoes on a day-to-day basis, but I never pass over ulster champ when in Ireland! I baked a pound cake, my husband's favorite dessert, in the shape of Ireland, and decorated it with depictions of the four courses the guys would be playing. It was a pleasant end to a very filling meal.

Rosemary-Cheddar Scones

This recipe is a combination of several scone recipes that I have experimented with over the years. I use a scone pan to bake in. This recipe makes 16 scones.

- 3 cups all-purpose flour
- 1 tablespoon baking powder
- 1 tablespoon sugar
- 2 teaspoons salt
- 2 tablespoons chopped fresh rosemary
- 1½ cups grated cheddar cheese
- 2 cups heavy cream
- 1 egg, beaten, mixed with 1 tablespoon water to create egg wash

Preheat oven to 400 degrees. Sift together the flour, baking powder, sugar, and salt. Add the rosemary and cheddar cheese, tossing well to combine. Stir in the cream with a fork until a sticky dough forms. Turn the dough onto a lightly floured surface and knead with floured hands and roll out. Cut into 16 wedges and arrange in a greased scone pan. Brush with the egg wash and bake for 20 minutes until golden brown. If you do not have a scone pan, bake on an ungreased baking sheet, leaving about ½ inch between scones. Serve hot.

NAPOLEON IVY

Wedgwood began production of its Napoleon Ivy pattern in 1815 and discontinued it in 2003. It features a cream-colored background with a border of ivy leaves, ranging from dark forest green to a lighter grassy green, and stems painted in such realistic detail that the texture of the foliage emerges. Josiah Wedgwood first introduced his cream-colored earthenware body in the 1760s, after perfecting the process and creating a new benchmark for all ceramics. He presented Queen Charlotte with a tea service in this new body, and she loved it so much that she asked him to call it Queen's Ware, which is what the style is still referred to as today. The mark on the backside of this pattern reads, "Napolean Ivy, as used by Napoleon at St. Helena, 1815, Wedgwood, England."

The dark oak antique Welsh Dresser that I often use to showcase my Napolean Ivy collection was one of my first antique pieces. It came with me to Chestnut Cottage and is very close to my heart. On the walls around it are menus that I have collected from restaurants I have enjoyed during my travels.

Josiah Wedgwood presented Queen Charlotte with a tea service, and she loved it so much that she asked him to call it Queen's Ware, which is what the style is still referred to as today.

ANTIQUE FISH CUTLERY

The Victorians were famous for having a serving piece for every imaginable function. During a time when showcasing personal wealth was of the utmost importance, the more elaborate a table setting, the better. In Victorian England the fish course consisted of a whole poached fish and was accompanied by a master set of fish cutlery, which included a large knife and fork for serving, and individual forks and knives for each place setting.

The sets featured in this event were found in England and Scotland—still in their original, velvet-lined boxes—and have handles of bone. One of the sets features a delicate ivy motif, which made this the perfect complement to the Napoleon Ivy pattern.

During the Victorian era, a time when showcasing personal wealth was of the utmost importance, the more elaborate a table setting, the better.

CHAPTER 9

HIGH-ON-THE-HOG BAR-B-QUE

*S*everal years ago, my very dear clients Doc and Katie Beatty approached me about throwing a party for their contractor and subs. I suggested that the party be held while the project was still in progress, perhaps before the drywall was put up and while the home maintained its construction-site feel. I felt the job site would be a unique venue for the party and would also add a level of comfort for the guests.

Since then, I have helped many of my new construction clients throw a similar party. There is something magical about celebrating in a partially completed house with those responsible for turning the project into a finished home. A construction site party is a special way to say thank you, not only to the crew who worked so hard but also to the families that supported them during the process.

There is something magical about celebrating in a partially completed house with those responsible for turning it into a home.

We planned this particular event on the construction site of my clients Mitch and Sue Levine's future second home in the mountains of western North Carolina. The lot boasts incredible views of majestic blue mountains layered in the distance and looks down on an old railroad track running alongside the meandering French Broad River. From their completed outdoor living space, the Levines would soon be able to watch rafters and river enthusiasts floating along the French Broad, but at the time they were ready to enjoy the process rather than the finished product. We decided against fancy food and pristine tables. The event would be a casual, mountain-style celebration called "High-on-the-Hog Bar-B-Que and Bluegrass."

In keeping with the theme of the event—and using Golden Rabbit's "Veneer" pattern for inspiration—I asked an antique dealer friend for a thin slice of mahogany to write the invitation on. I attached the veneer to the construction site message board for all the workers to see. The message board is the communications center on a construction site and holds permits and other pertinent information. I thought it would be a nice way to share the event with those invited.

"Lay down your hard hats, hammers, and saws. Bring your appetites, family, and all! Join the Levines for an evening of 'High-on-the-Hog BBQ' and Bluegrass, Saturday, July 10th, five o'clock p.m."

Sawhorses topped with sheets of plywood made up the tables, and benches were created from lumber and concrete blocks collected onsite. These were set up in the place that would become the family's outdoor living area. I draped burlap tablecloths over the plywood tables for a casually "elegant" look. Striped, woven napkins brought construction site hues to the tables: tan, brown, green, and rust. I tied them with a simple green string I use in the garden at Chestnut Cottage. A pattern of bronze twig cutlery enhanced the casual outdoor theme.

I draped burlap tablecloths over plywood tables for a casually "elegant" look.

FOR PLACE CARDS I USED SLATE PIECES TIED WITH ROPE AND WOOD INSCRIBED WITH THE NAMES OF EACH WORKER.

Wildflowers collected from the roadside around the site were arranged in paint buckets that reflected the colors the Levines had chosen for the interior of the house. I added summer zinnias and coneflowers from the garden at Chestnut Cottage to complete the arrangements.

For place cards I used slate pieces tied with rope and wood, and wrote the names of the workers on each. Not knowing the names of the wives and children who were to attend, I used the place cards in a nontraditional manner, to honor and recognize the men on the job site rather than to hold place settings for guests.

What goes better on a job site with beer than popcorn and pretzels? We served casual hors d'oeuvres in old wooden dough bowls and nail boxes. We made cones out of old blue prints for individual servings of popcorn, and the cold beer was served up in an antique copper boiler. The workers and their families delighted in a meal of Bar-B-Que, broccoli coleslaw, potato salad, three-bean baked beans, and hushpuppies. We also served delicious homemade peach ice cream, churned right on the job site, in the Veneer mugs with cookies from Blue Ridge Bakery (a client of mine who bakes my company's Signature Shortbread cookies).

What goes better on a job site than beer, popcorn, and pretzels?

I wanted the favors to be something that the guys would get a great deal of use out of and decided on custom-designed ball caps and T-shirts that congratulated the contractors and subs for a job well done. The fronts of the T-shirts boasted the logos of all the team members: the architectural firm, Platt and Associates, of Brevard, North Carolina; Kathryn Greeley Designs of Waynesville; and Sullbark Construction Company, the general contractors on this project.

The architect of the project, Al Platt, has two very talented sons. Parker Platt is an architect in his father's firm, and Woody Platt is a member of the internationally acclaimed bluegrass band Steep Canyon Rangers. The personal connection between our project and the bluegrass band made our evening of bar-b-que and bluegrass all the more special, and we played Steep Canyon Ranger CDs for the evening's entertainment.

An evening of live bluegrass and beer makes for a very happy construction crew. A job well done celebrated high on the hog!

HIGH-ON-THE-HOG
BAR-B-QUE MENU

Beer, Popcorn, and Pretzels

~~~

BBQ

~~~

Broccoli Coleslaw

~~~

Potato Salad

~~~

Three-Bean Baked Beans

~~~

Hushpuppies

~~~

Homemade Peach Ice Cream
and Cookies

Broccoli Slaw

3 Bean Baked Beans

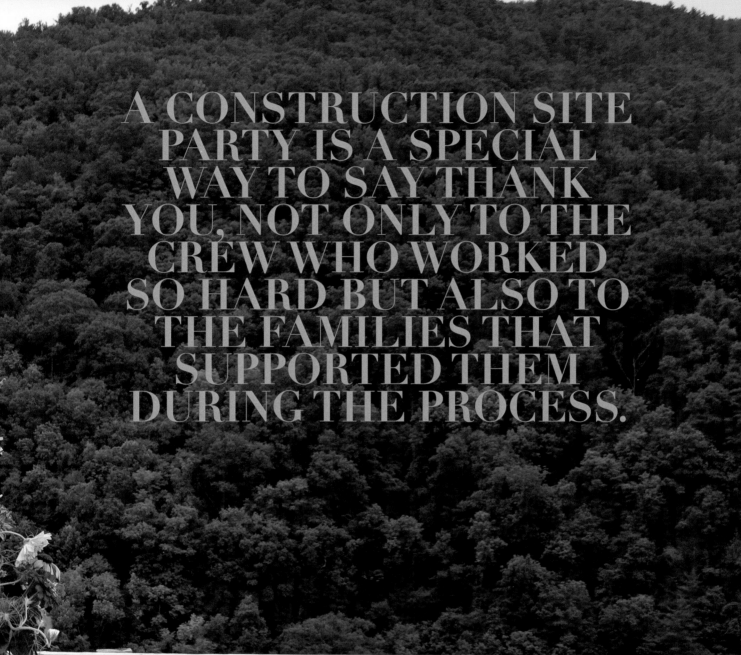

A CONSTRUCTION SITE PARTY IS A SPECIAL WAY TO SAY THANK YOU, NOT ONLY TO THE CREW WHO WORKED SO HARD BUT ALSO TO THE FAMILIES THAT SUPPORTED THEM DURING THE PROCESS.

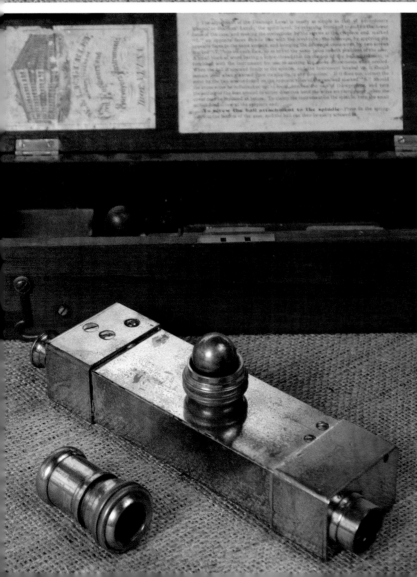

ANTIQUE TOOLS

My friends Larry Clark and Ron Leatherwood, owners of Clark and Leatherwood Construction in Waynesville, North Carolina, have a fascinating and valuable collection of antique construction tools, and they were kind enough to share these with me for this event. Many of these tools were used before the time when electricity was even an option on a construction site. Due to the higher grade of materials used in the past, older construction tools are usually considered superior to many of today's tools.

The books displayed on one of the tables make up a complete four-volume set of Audels Masons & Builders guidebooks, published and printed by Theo. Audel & Co of New York, first copyrighted in 1924 and reprinted in 1950.

The antique drainage level, circa 1899, by W. & L. E. Gurley of Troy, New York, is an early predecessor of today's transits and building levels. This American artifact is sold at today's auctions for hundreds of dollars.

WITH TODAY'S TECHNOLOGY AND METHODS OF MEASUREMENT, IT IS HARD TO IMAGINE THE IMPORTANCE PLACED ON THESE SIMPLE ANTIQUE TOOLS.

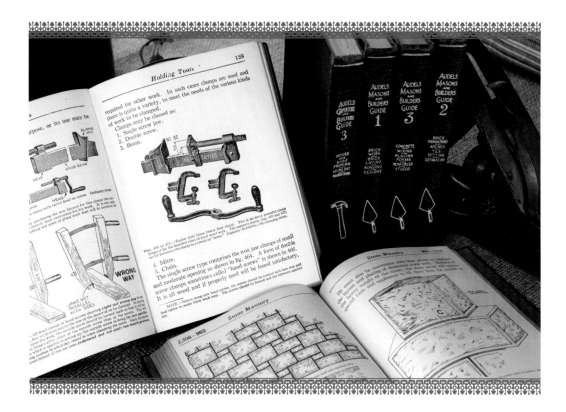

The books displayed on one of the tables make up a complete four-volume set of Audels Masons & Builders guidebooks, first copyrighted in 1924.

At the time Stanley Folding Rules were being produced, they were considered the most essential tools for those whose work required precision and accuracy. They were made in unique measurements and graduations for use not only by carpenters but by milliners, tailors, and carriage makers as well. With today's technology and methods of measurement, it is hard to imagine the importance placed on these simple antique tools. And while present-day carpenters would not choose to use such archaic tools, there is a high demand for these folding rules by antique tool enthusiasts. Those displayed fold out to 6-foot and 12-foot lengths and are most likely made of boxwood, though it was not uncommon for these rules to be made of ivory as well.

This collection also features antique braces, hand drills, and a fence/molding plane originally used to hand-cut crown moldings. A personal favorite of mine is the old cloth nail pouch; its simplicity and functionality are still present in today's construction needs, making it a rarity among antique building supplies.

REPRODUCTION ENAMELWARE

After searching for an old tinware dinnerware service to no avail, I settled on Veneer, by Golden Rabbit, a unique collection inspired by eighteenth-century tinware designs and perfectly suited for this event. Designer Tom Newbury of Art and Commerce Designs developed this masculine, rustic pattern for Golden Rabbit.

The porcelain enamel products feature the unique look and feel of tin plates but are superior to tin in almost every other way. The high-temperature firing methods used to create the collections of Golden Rabbit allow the pieces to be used for baking and stove-top cooking, and they are also dishwasher safe. The high-grade steel and porcelain products used to manufacture this enamelware are safe for food service and far outlast the typical tin plate.

Broccoli Coleslaw

- 2 bags (12 ounces) broccoli coleslaw mix
- 1½ cups dried cranberries
- ¾ cups toasted pine nuts
- 3 Gala or Granny Smith apples, seeded, and cut into small chunks
- 1–1½ cups Brianna's Poppy Seed Dressing

Mix first four ingredients and then toss with the desired amount of dressing.

Three-Bean Baked Beans

- ⚜ 10 slices lean bacon
- ⚜ 1 large onion, chopped
- ⚜ 1 large green bell pepper, chopped
- ⚜ 1½ cups catsup
- ⚜ 1 cup BBQ sauce
- ⚜ ½ cup yellow mustard
- ⚜ 1 cup brown sugar
- ⚜ 1 16-ounce can cannellini beans, drained and rinsed
- ⚜ 1 16-ounce can red kidney beans, drained and rinsed
- ⚜ 1 32-ounce can of pork and beans, drained and rinsed

Brown four slices of the bacon. Remove from pan and set aside. In the bacon grease, sauté the onions and pepper. In a large mixing bowl, mix the catsup, BBQ sauce, mustard, brown sugar, and beans. Crumble the four slices of cooked bacon and add to the mixture, along with the onions and peppers. Mix well. Pour into a 9-inch x 13-inch baking dish and arrange six slices of bacon on the top. Bake at 350 degrees for 45 minutes.

Signature Shortbread Cookies

A wonderful young woman in my community, Nancy East, is a trained veterinarian. When her children were born she decided to stay at home and do something that she was passionate about—baking! I knew her to be a wonderful and loving vet when she cared for my precious Bentley Greeley, so I imagined she would also be a great baker. I employed Nancy to bake cookies anytime we needed them at Kathryn Greeley Designs, and then I decided that we needed our own signature cookies as a treat for clients. Nancy researched and found a company that custom made cookie stamps. Now we have our own signature shortbread cookies! I would like to share Nancy's recipe with you.

- ✦ 1½ cups butter
- ✦ ¾ cup sugar
- ✦ 3½ cups all-purpose, unbleached flour

Cream the butter and sugar thoroughly. Add flour gradually, one cup at a time. Mix until well blended, but do not overmix. Roll into 1-inch balls and place on an ungreased cookie sheet. Stamp with a cookie stamp. Bake at 350 degrees in a preheated oven for 15 minutes or until lightly brown.

CHAPTER 10

FALL FOR FOOTBALL

My dear friends and clients Ron and Laura Leatherwood completed work on a new, outdoor living space at their home in Waynesville, North Carolina, just in time for this event. I have worked with them on several additions to their home over the years, and it was a joy to be involved in the most recent. We put the finishing touches on the design just in time for football season, Ron's favorite time of the year. An official in the Southeastern Conference for many years, Ron truly loves all things football, and I felt that football would be the ideal theme for an event designed to christen their new outdoor living space and gather friends together. This was one of the few weekends that he was not officiating, and he was able to relax with his feet up and enjoy watching the game rather than being in the thick of it all.

The newly constructed outdoor living room is quite large with a square dining table that seats eight. I prefer this shape rather than a rectangular table because it allows for much more inclusive and intimate conversation. There is a large seating area around the fireplace, above which hangs a flat screen television. The mantle is made of wormy chestnut and the fireplace surround is made of stone native to Western North Carolina. The morning of the event I didn't have to search far for red and gold leaves to cover the mantle and fill an old copper piece on the hearth.

I LOVE SQUARE TABLES BECAUSE THEY ALLOW FOR MORE INCLUSIVE AND INTIMATE CONVERSATION.

I used a combination of wicker, reclaimed wood furniture, and metal in the design of this open-air room to add depth through various textures. The seating area around the fireplace and the dining area both feature very colorful kilim rugs, Sunbrella fabrics treated for outdoor use, and outdoor lamps.

The guest powder room of this home is filled with Ron's memorabilia collected over the years he has spent officiating football. It is truly one of his great loves, and I thought it appropriate to honor Ron and something that means so much to him by displaying this collection prominently in their home.

A very simple invitation asked friends to join the Leatherwoods in christening their new outdoor living space. The text was printed on vellum and tied to a rust-colored, textured handmade paper with a deeper rust-colored ribbon. The menu for the evening was printed and designed to mimic the invitation with a combination of vellum, handmade paper, and ribbon.

The guest powder room of this home is filled with Ron's memorabilia collected over the years he has spent officiating football.

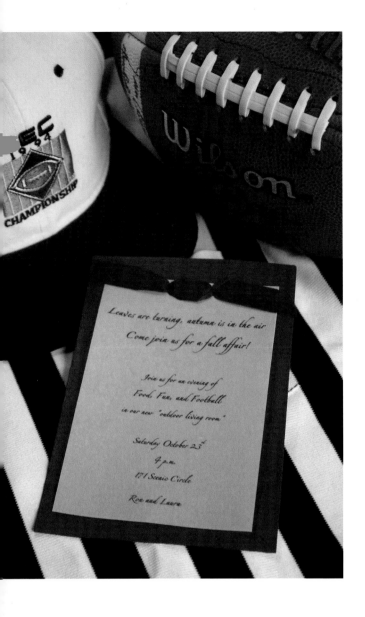

Leaves are turning, autumn is in the air
Come join us for a fall affair!

Join us for an evening of
Food, Fun, and Football
in our new "outdoor living room"

Saturday October 23rd

4 p.m.

171 Scenic Circle

Ron and Laura

BOTH THE MENU AND THE INVITATION FEATURE A COMBINATION OF VELLUM, HANDMADE PAPER, AND RIBBON.

This evening's tablescape included a collection of majolica and a set of hand-thrown pottery dinnerware. I covered the square metal table with a gold quilted tablecloth and folded moss-green linen napkins to accentuate the greens in the majolica pieces that were a part of the setting. I chose a set of bronze cutlery with twig handles that enhanced the twig embellishment on Brad's hand-thrown salad plates. What was most unique about the table were the various shapes of the pottery pieces and the contrast of this earth-toned, casual dinner service with the bright and the more formal majolica. In Brad's collection, no one piece is exactly alike in color or texture. On the tabletop, the round dinner plate, with its "sideboards," embraced the salad plate and the leaf soup bowl.

The place cards were simply scripted names on handmade paper placed to the right of each setting.

The centerpiece consisted of wooden candlesticks, several pitchers, and other pieces of Laura's majolica collection. The pitchers were overflowing with roses, sunflowers, and other fall flowers that reflected the vibrant colors present across the mountains of North Carolina during autumn, and accented the colors in the majolica pieces.

The tablescape included a collection of majolica and a set of hand-thrown pottery dinnerware.

Menu

Fall Apple Salad

Clam Chowder

Broccoli Cornbread

S'Mores Crème Brûlée

What was unique about this table was the contrast of this earth-toned, casual dinner service with the bright and more formal majolica pottery.

Hors d'oeuvres were served in a collection of pottery serving pieces that Brad had previously made for the client as well as a few he had made specifically for this event, including a freeform leaf and one that resembles the soup bowl's leaf style. Smaller leaf bowls were used for condiments and guacamole. The game foods consisted of sausage pinwheels, cheese patties cut into the shape of fall leaves, an olive spread served with crackers, and a very large bowl of chips.

FALL FOR FOOTBALL MENU

Fall Apple Salad

Clam Chowder

Broccoli Cornbread

S'mores Crème Brûlée

Clam Chowder

I have been making this delicious chowder for years thanks to my old friends Tommy and Margaret Cogdill from Sylva, North Carolina. Including this recipe brings back memories of fun cooking and entertaining with this couple. I always double this recipe; the leftovers are great!

- ✝ 8 strips lean bacon, fried and crumbled
- ✝ 1 large onion, diced
- ✝ ½ teaspoon red pepper flakes
- ✝ 4 large potatoes, peeled and diced
- ✝ ½ pound whole clams, undrained
- ✝ ½ pound minced clams, undrained
- ✝ 1 can cream of celery soup (10¾ ounces)
- ✝ 1 can evaporated milk (12 ounces)

Fry the bacon in a stockpot until crisp. Remove the bacon and set aside. Brown the diced onion in the bacon drippings. Add red pepper flakes and potatoes. Cover with water and cook until the potatoes are soft. Add clams and simmer about 7 minutes. Add soup and evaporated milk. Simmer 45 minutes. Salt and pepper to taste. Top with crumbled bacon just before serving.

Broccoli Cornbread

This is another wonderful recipe left to me by my mother-in-law, Miriam Greeley. Often, I double the recipe and fix it in a 9-inch x 13-inch pan, but normally I make it in my cast-iron frying pan.

- 1 medium onion, chopped
- ½ cup chopped red bell pepper
- ½ cup chopped green or yellow bell pepper
- 1 stick butter, melted
- 10-ounce package frozen chopped broccoli, thawed and patted dry
- 6 ounces cottage cheese
- 4 eggs, beaten
- 1 teaspoon salt
- 1½ cups grated cheddar cheese
- 8½-ounce box Jiffy Cornbread Mix
- Optional: chopped jalapeno peppers to taste

Sauté onions and peppers in Pam or a small amount of butter. Combine all ingredients. Bake in a lightly greased 8-inch x 8-inch pan at 400 degrees for 30–40 minutes or until golden brown. Check for doneness with a toothpick.

Knowing that we would first spend the afternoon watching football and munching on delicious hors d'oeuvres, I thought it best to keep the menu simple: a fall apple salad, clam chowder, and broccoli cornbread. The clam chowder recipe was given to me years ago by my friends and clients Tommy and Margaret Cogdill of Sylva, North Carolina. The broccoli cornbread recipe was left to me by my mother-in-law, Miriam Greeley. I prepare it in a black cast-iron cornbread pan, and it is a staple at our home every fall and winter.

A very special dessert of s'mores crème brûlée was served around the fireplace after dinner. This is a recipe that I learned when I attended the Aspen Cooking School years ago, and it has been a favorite of my friends and family ever since. Dessert was served on

I placed the delectable chocolates in a variety of small pottery leaves that Brad designed for each guest to use to take their treats home.

a set of antique majolica plates that worked perfectly with French crème brûlée ramekins. As opposed as I was to Ron's suggestion of using a plumber's torch rather than my kitchen torch, I stuck to my business theory that the client is always right, and we ended up with unevenly broiled marshmallows.

The Chocolate Fetish in Asheville, North Carolina, hand crafted chocolate-covered caramels with sea salt for the favor at this event. I placed the delectable chocolates in a variety of small pottery leaves that Brad designed for each guest to use to take their treats home. I noticed that several guests left with empty leaves, having devoured their sea salt caramels!

Before the guests left, we spent a few minutes by the fire to take in the crisp fall air and watch the full moon rise across a breathtaking evening sky, which was transitioning from deep blue to shades of pink and purple.

HAND-THROWN POTTERY

I commissioned potter Brad Dodson, owner of Mud Dabber's Pottery in Balsam, North Carolina, to design a set of dinnerware that would include many different shapes and forms. He created a square bread-and-butter plate, a round dinner plate with what he called "side boards" to hold lots of goodies, and a free-form salad plate with a twig depiction. My favorite piece in the collection is the deep soup bowl he designed in the shape of fall leaves. This hand-thrown pottery collection was executed in the colors of the mountains in fall and proved to be a beautiful addition to the Leatherwood's outdoor living space.

The Dodson family has been making pottery together since the 1970s. Truly a family business, the pottery of Mud Dabber's features the work of many family members and friends. John and his wife, Sybil, opened the first shop outside of Brevard, North Carolina. John E. and his wife, Carol, currently run the shop, which is now located in historic downtown Brevard. Brad, another of John and Sybil's sons, opened a second location in Balsam, just outside of Waynesville.

The art of throwing pottery begins quite simply with a ball of clay and a potter's wheel. The magic comes with the artist's imagination and ability to throw, fire, and glaze each ball of clay into a beautiful and original piece.

This hand-thrown pottery collection was executed in the colors of the mountains in fall and complements the outdoor living space.

MAJOLICA

Many collectors are hesitant to use pieces from their beloved collections, especially one as fine as Laura's majolica. Laura and I have been building this collection for years, and I displayed much of it in an antique console that has wire doors. Upon entering the Leatherwood's front door, one is greeted with the bright colors of the majolica set against a deep red wall. While building Laura's collection, I looked for pitchers that she could use for flower arrangements and both cake and compote stands for service of a variety of foods when entertaining.

What originally separated Victorian majolica from all other forms of pottery was its vibrant color and detailed depictions. It is still unparalleled today. During the Victorian era, importance was placed on beauty before usefulness, and as the bold and romantic times of the era faded away, so did the popularity of this exquisite pottery. A more conservative age was on the rise, and with it came a preference for more subtle pieces. The twentieth-century concept, form follows function, would not allow for the whimsical decoration of this vibrant pottery. During this time, majolica was viewed as excessive and outrageous, and the pieces lost favor among collectors.

Majolica brought beauty and finery into the homes of England's middle class during a time when all things vibrant and beautiful, such as porcelain, were reserved solely for the wealthy.

Majolica is a soft earthenware that is formed in molds of plaster of paris and fired in a kiln at a high temperature. The molds are then removed and the raw pieces are covered with a thin layer of lead-based glaze. When the glaze has dried, the piece is painted with colorful, metal oxide glazes. The interaction of the initial lead glaze with those painted on top of it during a second firing at a lower temperature creates the vivid, brilliant color attributed to majolica.

Thomas Minton of Staffordshire, England, introduced his majolica wares to Queen Victoria and the public at the Crystal Palace Exhibition in London in 1851, and its popularity rose and continued to grow for the next half century. By the late 1800s, majolica could be found in households on both sides of the Atlantic Ocean, regardless of social class.

Notable makers of majolica include Minton, of course, as well as Wedgwood, Holdcroft, and George Jones. The most widely recognized American makers of majolica are Griffin, Smith, and Hill and Chesapeake Pottery.

THE TERM *MAJOLICA* REFERS TO THE METHOD USED TO CREATE IT, NOT THE COMPANY THAT PRODUCED IT OR THE COUNTRY IN WHICH IT IS MADE. IF IT'S MADE WITHIN CERTAIN PARAMETERS, IT'S MAJOLICA, WHETHER IT WAS CREATED IN ENGLAND, GERMANY, OR AMERICA.

S'mores Crème Brûlée

For many years while my husband and friends skied in Aspen, I attended the Cooking School of Aspen. I always came home with lots of great recipes, and this is one of my favorites! It is a bit time-consuming, but it's well worth the effort.

- 2 egg yolks
- ¼ cup sugar
- ½ teaspoon pure vanilla extract
- Chocolate ganache
- 14 ounces semisweet chocolate
- 1 cup heavy cream

Whip together egg yolks, sugar, and vanilla. Heat chocolate ganache, semisweet chocolate, and heavy cream together using the top of a double boiler until chocolate is melted. Slowly add mixtures together and stir. Cool. Spread on the bottom of eight brûlée dishes.

Crème Brûlée

- 2 cups heavy cream
- 2 cups whole milk
- ¾ cup sugar
- 16 egg yolks
- 1 vanilla pod, scraped

Bring cream and milk to a soft boil in a saucepan. Whisk together sugar and egg yolks with the vanilla pod until blended. Slowly add the milk mixture to the egg yolk mixture and return to low heat for 6–8 minutes, stirring until thick. Pour over ganache in each of the brûlée dishes. Top with graham-cracker-crumb mixture. Serves eight.

Graham Cracker Crumbs

+ 16 ounces graham cracker crumbs
+ 2 sticks melted butter
+ 1 teaspoon cinnamon
+ 4 tablespoons sugar

Combine all ingredients in a food processor. Sprinkle graham-cracker-crumb mixture on top of the ganache and top with mini marshmallows. Set under the broiler until golden brown or brown with a kitchen torch. Garnish with a graham cracker.

CHAPTER 11

INDEPENDENCE DAY LAKESIDE CELEBRATION

My husband and I are blessed to have a second home at the beautiful Lake Chatuge, nestled in the mountains of Western North Carolina and North Georgia. This has been a family residence for two generations, and there is nowhere else I would rather spend my summers. Each year we host a Fourth of July house party to gather together family and friends and celebrate our country's Independence Day. Golfing, swimming, boating, reading, and, most important, relaxing are the main events during this long weekend of food, fun, and fireworks.

I kept the invitation for this event simple and festive, with the American flag boldly printed on either side. The text, in different fonts, over the red and white stripes, created a fun and celebratory feeling, just what I wanted my guests to experience when they opened the envelope.

"FREEDOM'S NATAL
DAY IS HERE,
FIRE THE GUNS
AND SHOUT FOR
FREEDOM,
SEE THE FLAG
ABOVE UNFURLED!
HAIL THE STARS
AND STRIPES
FOREVER,
DEAREST FLAG IN
ALL THE WORLD."

—FLORENCE A. JONES

The evening began with a cocktail cruise on the gorgeous mountain lake. My favorite mode of lake transportation belongs to my great friend Randy Cunningham, whose restored 1965 Philbrick wooden runabout is named Junaluska after the lake he lives on in Waynesville, North Carolina. We packed up the vintage quilt and wicker hamper we had used during lakeshore cocktails and climbed aboard. I discovered this quilt, along with a forty-eight-state flag and a group of small vintage flags first flown at Arlington Cemetery, at a favorite antique shop in Hayesville, North Carolina, called "Molly and Me."

We kicked off the evening with a cocktail cruise on the lake.

The centerpiece overflowed with delphiniums, hydrangeas, zinnias, and vintage flags from Arlington Cemetery.

There are never enough beach towels during these weekends, so I decided to give American flag beach towels as favors to each of our guests. I tied the towels on the back of each chair as I dressed the lakeside tables arranged for dinner on the lower lawn. I chose a red-and-white-checked Ralph Lauren fabric for the tablecloth, overlaid with a solid blue undercloth. The combination complemented the red, white, and blue plaid Calico pattern wonderfully. New cobalt blue chargers with ruffled edges were a recent birthday gift, and they hugged the Calico pieces beautifully. For this tabletop, I placed a casual blue cloth napkin directly under the Calico lugged chowder bowls. I opted for no place cards at this casual lakeside meal. The table was completed with cobalt blue water glasses and several small "beehive" vases filled with red, white, and blue flowers. The centerpiece was a large cobalt blue vase made by Morganton Glass Works circa 1940, which overflowed with blue delphiniums, blue and white hydrangeas, red zinnias, and the vintage flags from Arlington Cemetery.

After a long cruise, dinner was served lakeside in our lower yard.

After a long cruise, dinner was served lakeside, in our lower yard, and the menu was the same as the year before. Each year my guests plead that I keep the same menu the following year. The main course is always short ribs and firecracker shrimp on skewers, and I make sure to offer extra BBQ sauce. My mother's potato salad, bacon-balsamic deviled eggs, baked beans, and grilled corn with basil butter are the sides of choice each Fourth of July. My family, friends, and I have come to view this as the quintessential lakeside cookout, and it delights year after year.

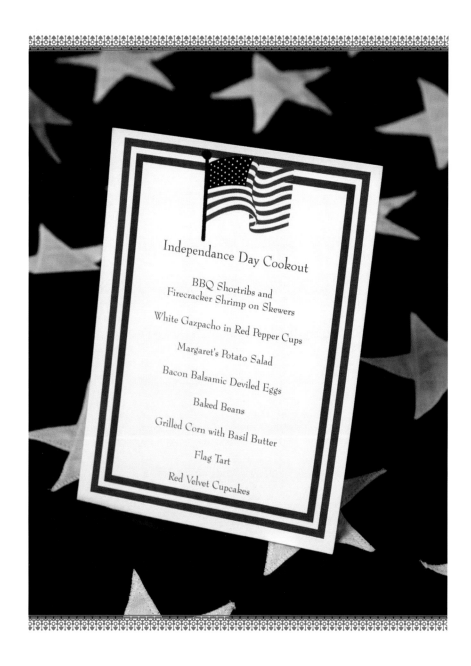

Independance Day Cookout

BBQ Shortribs and
Firecracker Shrimp on Skewers

White Gazpacho in Red Pepper Cups

Margaret's Potato Salad

Bacon Balsamic Deviled Eggs

Baked Beans

Grilled Corn with Basil Butter

Flag Tart

Red Velvet Cupcakes

WE ENJOYED TIME ON THE LAKE, LAUGHED, AND FILLED UP ON AN ARRAY OF FOODS WE HAD BEEN LOOKING FORWARD TO SINCE LAST YEAR.

Guests are generally stuffed after dinner, and we often wait for a while before enjoying dessert in the comfy wicker rockers on our deck overlooking the lake. My Red Velvet cakes are famous among my family and in my community. For the Independence Day celebration, I turned them into individual cupcakes and served them alongside a flag tart made with fresh berries and my homemade pudding recipe.

We enjoyed time on the lake, laughed, and filled up on an array of foods we had been looking forward to since last year. What a fantastic way to start the Independence Day Lakeside Celebration!

INDEPENDENCE DAY LAKESIDE CELEBRATION

BBQ Short Ribs

Firecracker Shrimp on Skewers

White Gazpacho in Red Pepper Cups

Margaret's Potato Salad

Bacon-Balsamic Deviled Eggs

Baked Beans

Grilled Corn with Basil Butter

Red Velvet Cupcakes

Independence Day Flag Tart

White Gazpacho

I usually put this recipe in scooped-out red pepper "cups,"
especially for my Fourth of July celebration.

- ✝ 2 cups low-sodium chicken broth
- ✝ 3 scallions, including the tops
- ✝ 1 tablespoon chopped fresh parsley
- ✝ 1 tablespoon chopped fresh tarragon
- ✝ 1 cup sour cream
- ✝ 1 cup plain yogurt
- ✝ 2 tomatoes, seeded and finely chopped
- ✝ 1 large English cucumber, peeled, seeded, and coarsely chopped
- ✝ ⅓ cup chopped green bell pepper
- ✝ Splash of sherry vinegar
- ✝ Fresh mint for garnishing

Place the first nine ingredients in the bowl of a food processor. Blend until smooth. Mix in the splash of sherry vinegar and refrigerate overnight. Before serving, you can process again if you prefer a smoother texture. Garnish with fresh mint.

Independence Day Flag Tart

Each Fourth of July I make this Independence Day flag tart. I start with a premade rolled pie crust (I use Pillsbury). I roll out the dough to a rectangle and fit it into an 8-inch x 11½-inch rectangular tart pan with a removable bottom. Bake the crust according to package directions. Cool crust completely and carefully remove crust from the tart pan. I top the cooled crust with a vanilla cream custard.

Vanilla Cream Custard

I use this delicious custard for a variety of desserts. I use it in my English Trifle and a variety of fruit tarts. It is also perfect with fresh fruit and cookies!

- ½ cup sugar
- ¼ cup cornstarch
- ¼ teaspoon salt
- 2 cups cold whole milk
- 4 egg yolks, lightly beaten
- 1 teaspoon pure vanilla extract

Combine the sugar, cornstarch, and salt in a saucepan. Add milk and egg yolks, stirring constantly with a whisk. Cook the mixture over medium heat until it comes to a low boil. Remove from heat and stir in the vanilla. Cool in the refrigerator.

I make a "flag" design over the custard using blueberries and raspberries or strawberries, and whipped cream to form the stars and stripes of the flag. Fresh-whipped cream can be piped from a pastry bag, or for a quicker option, I have used Reddi-wip.

WE OFTEN WAIT FOR A WHILE BEFORE ENJOYING DESSERT IN THE COMFY WICKER ROCKERS ON OUR DECK OVERLOOKING THE LAKE.

Kathryn's Red Velvet Cake

About thirty years ago, my neighbor Mary Worley gave me this recipe. Through the years I have seen dozens of red velvet cake recipes, all of which had cocoa powder as an ingredient. I have never tried any of them because I get rave reviews from this recipe. Lately, I have wondered if maybe Mary left the cocoa out by mistake. I don't really care because I truly love this version.

- 2 eggs
- 1½ cups sugar
- 1½ cups oil (I use canola oil)
- 1 teaspoon white vinegar
- 2½ cups cake flour (I prefer Swans Down)
- 1 teaspoon soda
- 1 cup buttermilk
- 1 teaspoon vanilla
- 1 1-ounce bottle red food coloring

Preheat oven to 350 degrees. Beat the eggs, adding sugar, oil, and vinegar. Sift flour and soda together. Add the flour to the egg mixture and then slowly add the buttermilk. Mix well and add vanilla and food coloring. Pour batter into a greased and floured 9-inch x 13-inch cake pan. Bake for 25–30 minutes until a toothpick comes out clean. Cool cake before icing.

Cream Cheese Icing

- 8 ounces cream cheese
- 1 stick butter
- 1 16-ounce box confectioner's sugar
- 1½ cups chopped pecans

Soften the cream cheese and butter to room temperature. Add the confectioner's sugar and beat the mixture until smooth. Spread on cooled cake and top with chopped pecans.

I often make this recipe as cupcakes. You will get approximately 30 cupcakes using ¼ cup of batter for each cupcake. If making cupcakes, bake for 15 minutes or until a toothpick comes out clean.

THE MOMENT A
NEW COLLECTION
BEGINS IS SPECIAL
FOR ANY TRUE
COLLECTOR OF
FINE THINGS.

CALICO

Growing up in the 1950s, I was fascinated by my mother's everyday dinnerware. It was an Ironstone plaid pattern of rust, green, and gold called "Homespun," made by Metlox/Poppytrail/Vernon of California, and manufactured between 1949 and 1955. I have countless memories of family meals served with this dinnerware. While searching for a few pieces of her old pattern at Replacements, Ltd., I discovered a pattern identical to my mother's except in color. Calico is the same plaid design in red, white, and blue. I immediately thought of our summer celebrations and knew this would be the perfect choice for entertaining at our lake house. The moment a new collection begins is special for any true collector of fine things, and I was thrilled to add this pattern to my lake house repertoire. It accented my Old British Castle pattern by Johnson Brothers brilliantly and made the perfect addition to our lake-house collections.

One of my favorite pieces of the Calico pattern is the lugged chowder bowl. These bowls allow for a beautiful presentation of my white gazpacho served in a hollowed-out red bell pepper.

COBALT BLUE GLASS

At the beginning of each summer I select pieces from my collection of cobalt blue glass at Chestnut Cottage to bring to the lake house. Because cobalt glass originated during America's Great Depression and was a method of creating functional items from otherwise wasted materials, the list of products made from this beautiful blue glass is wide ranging: plates and glasses, of course, as well as cake stands, like mine made by The Hazel-Atlas Glass Company, circa 1930, but also milk jugs, rolling pins, and other more unusual necessities of the time. I always bring along my collection of cobalt blue vases, such as the ribbed beehive vases, unattributed to any maker, circa 1930. My collection features tumblers, bowls, and plates made by both The Hazel-Atlas Glass Company and The Cambridge Glass Company, circa 1930–1950. One of my favorite pieces is a small milk jug from Liberty Milk Company of Buffalo, New York. The Baker's Choice vintage rolling pin was used to roll the dough for the Flag Tart dessert.

One of my favorite pieces is a milk jug from Liberty Milk Company of Buffalo, New York.

CHAPTER 12

CELEBRATING THANKSGIVING DAY TRADITIONS

Thanksgiving is a very special time of year for my family. I am grateful for my many blessings, and I appreciate this day that was set aside for us to take time out of our busy lives and focus on all that we have to be thankful for.

For many years, Wells and I have opened Chestnut Cottage to our family, friends, and "strays," as I lovingly call new friends who may not have a place to celebrate this holiday. We share our home and the holiday each year because we are grateful for the blessing of a warm house, delicious food, and special family and friends. Our Thanksgiving celebration at Chestnut Cottage is a gift from Wells and me to the special people in our lives, and I work hard each year to make sure that it will be an unforgettable day. No guests are allowed to bring a single item; I ask only that they come and share in the holiday with us and accept this meal as an offering of gratitude and appreciation.

"BE NOT FORGETFUL TO
ENTERTAIN STRANGERS:
FOR THEREBY SOME
HAVE ENTERTAINED
ANGELS UNAWARE."

—HEBREWS 13:2

On holidays past, my paternal grandmother Janie Crisp cooked tremendous meals for her large extended family and many guests. One dessert was never enough; she generally offered up to five for each dinner, one of which, without fail, was her famous caramel cake, a recipe that most likely originally came out of a farm journal. I have noticed that similar recipes are most always in the possession of women of her generation. Grandmother Crisp was a countrywoman who relished her vegetable and flower gardens and shared her home and food with many. She remains one of my greatest inspirations for entertaining.

For our Thanksgiving invitation I chose a simple vellum overlay over a mossy-green scalloped border. On the invitation I scripted the message Wells and I believe most reflects the meaning of the holiday.

I tied the invitations to jars of my homemade lime pickles and attached an antique pickle fork to each one. Upon receiving this invitation, our guests also got a taste of what was to come!

"We are grateful for our home, our food, our family, our friends!"

One of my favorite things about the design of Chestnut Cottage is the open flow, which perfectly facilitates my frequent entertaining. Even with a group as large as twenty-four to thirty people, I enjoy the fact that the mealtime conversation spills over, from table to table, and later throughout the rooms. I set the reproduction table, made from reclaimed lumber from England, in my kitchen, an antique table in our gathering room, and an extra table that seats up to ten in the open area of our master bedroom. My guests feel comfortable moving around, visiting other tables, and the laughter can be heard from each of the three tables. Rarely does one end up in the same seat throughout the meal, and coffee and dessert are often enjoyed with other friends.

One of my most cherished antique pieces is the heavily carved dark oak sideboard. Day-to-day it features pieces of my silver collection, but on Thanksgiving, I use it for the dessert offerings.

One of my most cherished antique pieces at Chestnut Cottage is the heavily carved dark oak sideboard. On a day-to-day basis it features pieces of my silver collection, but on days such as Thanksgiving, I use it to serve my grandmother's caramel cake along with other dessert offerings such as pecan tarts and pumpkin pies.

Butter pats in Thanksgiving-themed shapes have become a tradition at Chestnut Cottage.

I chose to start with a bare tabletop to make the most of the contrast between the dark oak table, the white linen place mats and napkins, and the blue and white of the Flow Blue china. The butter pat dishes just above the salts have become a special tradition at Chestnut Cottage. For years, my young friends, the Morris children, have prepared cut butter pats in Thanksgiving-themed shapes to be placed in the small Flow Blue dishes at each setting. A Flow Blue bone dish sits above the dinner plate. I chose to use the small and large wine glasses as well as the champagne flute from my collection of William Yeoward's crystal in the Pearl pattern for our Thanksgiving cheer. Small Limoges pumpkin boxes served as place card holders and introduced a touch of fall color to the table.

OUR THANKSGIVING FAVOR: HANDMADE CHOCOLATE TURKEYS NESTLED IN A CLEAR BOX.

My friends at the nationally known chocolatier The Chocolate Fetish in Asheville, North Carolina, designed our Thanksgiving favor: handmade chocolate turkeys with tail feathers painted in yellow, orange, and red, nestled lovingly in a clear box and placed at the seat of each of our guests.

I arranged a variety of sizes from my collection of barley twist candlesticks on the table. This informal look created a perfect balance alongside a single, large Flow Blue vessel that sat in the center of the table, overflowing with Bells of Ireland, fall-colored roses, and, rich, blue delphiniums. A notable fact about Flow Blue China is that some patterns are much more formal than others, and a solid collection is made up of both varieties. I like to mix both on the same table setting. Upon completion, I had designed a Thanksgiving table that was formal and elegant but also comfortable and inviting. Each table had a variety of Flow Blue patterns from several English manufacturers.

CELEBRATING THANKSGIVING

Goat Cheese with Pepper
Jelly on Crispy Spoon-
Shaped Crackers

Cranberry Conserve
and Cranberry
Congealed Salad

Roast Turkey with
Cornbread Dressing
and Oyster Dressing

Glazed Baked Ham
with Pineapple Rings

Green Beans

Sweet Potatoes in
Orange "Cups"

Pineapple Soufflé

Broccoli Casserole

Mashed Potatoes
with Gravy

Pinch Bread

Caramel Cake

Pecan Pie Tarts

Maple Pumpkin Pies

Lime Pickles

- ‡ 2 cups pickling lime
- ‡ 2 gallons water
- ‡ 5 quarts unpeeled cucumbers, cut approximately ¼-inch thick
- ‡ 2 quarts white vinegar
- ‡ 9 cups sugar
- ‡ 1 teaspoon salt
- ‡ 1 teaspoon celery seed
- ‡ 1 teaspoon whole cloves
- ‡ 1 teaspoon pickling spice
- ‡ ½ of a 1-ounce bottle green food coloring

Dissolve the pickling lime in the two gallons of water in a ceramic crock. Let the cucumbers stand in the crock for 24 hours, stirring frequently. After 24 hours, rinse the cucumbers until the water is clear. Place in ice water and let stand for 3 hours. Drain well. In a large pot, mix the vinegar, sugar, salt, spices, and food coloring. Add the cucumbers to this mixture and let stand overnight. The following morning, cook the cucumbers in the vinegar mixture at a slow boil for 35 minutes. Jar the cucumbers at once, cover with the cooking liquid, and seal at once.

We enjoyed a traditional Thanksgiving menu of turkey and dressing, gravy, and baked ham.

Just before Thanksgiving every year, my husband teases that I should consider changing the menu a bit. One of our frequent Thanksgiving guests replied that there may well be a rebellion of the patrons if this were to occur!

I chose a traditional Thanksgiving menu of turkey and dressing, gravy, and baked ham. Mother and I enjoy our tradition of being together the Tuesday evening before each Thanksgiving to make my grandmother's dressing recipe. A favorite childhood memory of mine is of my mother and her friends using scooped-out orange peels piled full of sweet potatoes for holiday parties, and I use this beautiful technique each Thanksgiving. My menu always includes a variety of vegetables, many of which, like my fresh green beans, were grown locally.

A highlight of Thanksgiving at Chestnut Cottage is my homemade pinch bread. Guests often lurk in the shadows at the close of the lunch, hoping for leftovers to take home along with a jar of my homemade strawberry freezer jam. But for my guests with a sweet tooth, the star of the meal is my grandmother's old-fashioned caramel cake.

Grandmother Crisp's Caramel Cake

This is the only recipe that I have from my paternal grandmother, Janie Crisp. She had a large family and was a wonderful cook and made so many scrumptious desserts. Over the years, I have seen similar recipes that belonged to women of her generation. I suspect that they originated in a farm journal of some type.

- ⁜ 3 sticks butter
- ⁜ 3 cups sugar
- ⁜ 5 eggs
- ⁜ 3½ cups all-purpose flour
- ⁜ ¼ teaspoon salt
- ⁜ ½ teaspoon baking powder
- ⁜ 1¼ cups whole milk
- ⁜ 1 teaspoon vanilla

Cream the butter, sugar, and eggs together and beat well. In a separate bowl, combine dry ingredients. Add the dry ingredients alternately with the milk, and then add vanilla. Beat in a mixer bowl or with a hand mixer until the batter "ribbons." Pour batter into three greased and floured 9-inch cake pans. Bake for about 30 minutes and check for doneness with a toothpick. This cake can also be made in a 9-inch x 13-inch sheet pan, which will need to be baked for about 45 minutes. Cool layers on a cake rack before icing.

Caramel Icing

- ✝ 2 sticks butter
- ✝ 1 16-ounce box of light brown sugar
- ✝ ¼ teaspoon salt
- ✝ 2 sticks butter
- ✝ ⅔ cup evaporated milk (canned)
- ✝ 2 cups sifted confectioner's sugar
- ✝ 2 teaspoons pure vanilla extract

Place butter, brown sugar, and salt in a saucepan. Heat, stirring until the brown sugar is dissolved well. Add milk and continue stirring until blended. Let bubble (at an easy boil) for about 4 minutes. Stir constantly to avoid sticking. Set hot mixture aside to cool for several minutes. Using mixer, add confectioner's sugar and vanilla. You will see it turn lighter and caramelize. When you've reached the desired consistency, ice the cake, placing some of the icing between layers.

FLOW BLUE

The collection of Flow Blue china at Chestnut Cottage has grown and evolved over the last thirty-plus years. It is now displayed in every room of our home. My most enduring passion for years has been the hunt for this fascinating pattern, and Flow Blue is now my most valuable china collection. I often joke with friends that my retirement account is held in Flow Blue.

The lime used in the firing process of Flow Blue is what gives this pattern its soft, melt-away look.

Flow Blue was first created in England in the early- to mid-1800s as a sturdier, less-expensive alternative to Chinese porcelain. It quickly became a popular technique with English potters because of the ease of transferring the printed, underglazed designs and the fact that the "flowing" of the blue

"THERE'S A JOY
WITHOUT CANKER
OR CORK, THERE'S
A PLEASURE
ETERNALLY NEW, 'TIS
TO GLOAT ON THE
GLAZE AND THE MARK
OF CHINA THAT IS
ANCIENT AND BLUE."

—ANDREW LANG,
"THE BALLAD OF BLUE CHINA"

Pinch Bread

- 2 packages dry yeast
- 1 cup warm water
- 1 cup boiling water
- 1 cup Crisco
- ¾ cup sugar
- 1½ teaspoons salt
- 2 eggs, beaten
- 6 cups all-purpose flour, sifted
- 1 stick butter, melted

Dissolve the yeast in the warm water and set aside. In a large bowl, combine the cup of boiling water with the cup of Crisco. Stir the hot water and Crisco until the Crisco is somewhat dissolved. Add the sugar, salt, and eggs. Sift the flour and then add to the Crisco mixture. Stir well. This mixture will be very stiff. Add the dissolved yeast and mix well. Cover and refrigerate overnight.

About three hours before baking, remove dough from the refrigerator and "punch the dough down." Separate the dough in half. Do not knead the dough. Roll out the dough about ½-inch thick. Cut the dough with a small biscuit cutter. Dip each "biscuit" into the melted butter. Arrange the biscuits in a circle in a bundt pan, each layer staggering over the one beneath. Repeat with the remaining dough in a second pan. Cover with a towel and let rise in a warm place for 3 hours. Bake at 350 degrees for 30 minutes. Turn the bread onto a plate, reverse again, and serve with the top up.

Overnight guests at Chestnut Cottage are treated to breakfast in bed with warm pumpkin bread served in my Flow Blue toast rack.

transfers hid most every imperfection on a vessel. The "flow" in these patterns was created by introducing lime into the firing process of the earthenwares, giving the patterns the softness and melt-away look Flow Blue is so famous for.

The production of Flow Blue spread from England to France, Germany, Holland, and eventually America. It became an affordable alternative to porcelain because it was fine and delicate enough for formal dinner parties. While some English critics of Flow Blue were harsh and unforgiving of the technique, the American people took an instant liking to the patterns and the price point, and by the late-nineteenth century, Flow Blue could be found in the homes of many Americans, regardless of economical or social status.

There are two distinct styles in these patterns that may help in the identification of true Flow Blue. The first and most predominate pattern has a distinctive border design and a separate central image. The second, called sheet patterns, features a single floral or marbled pattern that covers a vessel in its entirety. Be sure to look for a maker's mark on the underside of each vessel. The marks are fascinating to study, and they tell the who, what, and where of each specific piece. The production of Flow Blue ended after the first quarter of the twentieth century. Today it is highly sought after by collectors of fine things.

As my most extensive and valuable china collection, Flow Blue was the natural choice for dinnerware as we gathered together for Thanksgiving with my most valuable collection in life—the family and friends I love!

One day, a few years ago, my friend Holly Morris called frantically from her home in Tampa, Florida, to tell me that she had come across quite a few pieces of Flow Blue that I might be interested in seeing. The dealer was in the process of downsizing and had an extensive collection of Flow Blue thanks to her collector mother and brother. Holly called the dealer and shared my story and then asked that she call me to discuss her Flow Blue collection.

We shared a long and tearful conversation about Flow Blue, and I understood her despair when she told me that she had been advised to sell her incredible collection on eBay. She felt that doing so would be heartbreaking as she had a strong need to see her family's very special collection fall into the hands of a collector who would appreciate it as much as she and her family had.

I visited her at her home in Florida and hand selected a hundred or so exquisite pieces of Flow Blue for several clients and myself. On an honest Flow Blue high, I purchased almost 80 percent of her collection and planned for its careful transport back to North Carolina. As we were leaving the dealer's home, Holly spotted a piece filled with plastic ivy that was sitting high atop an armoire. Taking the opportunity, she secretly purchased the cachepot and kept it for my husband to give to me as a future gift. Holly Morris seems to be my husband's personal shopper when it comes to antiques!

Americans took an instant liking to Flow Blue, and by the late-nineteenth century it could be found throughout the country regardless of social status.

ANTIQUE STERLING ENGLISH SALTS

Most of the antique salts in my collection were given to me by my designer friends Ed Springs and Bo Henderson. The majority came to me still in their lovely original satin or velvet-lined leather boxes. As the collection grew over the years, I began hunting for sterling salt spoons in a variety of patterns. My salts collection varies from very ornate, detailed patterns to very simple, classic patterns. Visitors to Chestnut Cottage are often awed by the ornate design of these small, delicate vessels. I use them in entertaining to feature a variety of sea salts that I enjoy cooking with.

WALLACE STERLING 4640-9

Margaret Pennington Roberts

CHESTNUT COTTAGE

*T*o say that I have always felt a deep connection with Chestnut Cottage is a bit of an understatement! The cottage beckoned to me the moment I crossed the threshold on my first visit. I was drawn in by the warmth and coziness, and knew it was always meant to be my adult home and quiet retreat. Chestnut Cottage nestles comfortably into the gently rolling landscape and simply has a strong sense of place—a place that has proven to be a collection of the fondest memories of my adult life. As an only child, home has always been a special place where I could be myself, nurture and express my hopes, dreams, and personal style, and share the gifts and talents that I have been blessed with.

I did not understand this strong, almost spiritual attraction that I felt to the cottage at the time I purchased it. My neighbors had told me that a lovely couple, Frank and Jesse Miller, had built the home and lived there before me. Every neighbor I spoke with confirmed my suspicion that the previous "lady of the house" loved the cottage just as I do. My curiosity about the previous owners led me to make a few further investigations; much to my surprise and delight, I learned that Mrs. Miller was from the very same small town as I, Bryson City, North Carolina! Though seemingly a coincidence, I believe that Mrs. Miller's joy and happiness left an imprint on the cottage that complemented my style and encouraged me to mold Chestnut Cottage's current personality. This new personality is built from my own memories, passions, family, and friends, and a lifetime of gathering and collecting.

RESOURCE GUIDE

The Best Entertaining Addresses from Chestnut Cottage

ANTIQUES

ACQUISITIONS LIMITED
2003 Fairview Road
Raleigh, NC 27608
919-755-1110
www.acquistionslimited.com

THE BIG CHANDELIER
484 14th Street, NW
Atlanta, GA 30318
404-872-3332
www.thebigchandelier.com

BLACK SHEEP ANTIQUES
336-432-0565 (by appointment only)

BURKE'S ANTIQUES
1030 Lexington Avenue
New York, NY 10021
212-570-2964

CLEMENTS ANTIQUES
OF TENNESSEE
7022 Highway 153
Hixson, TN 37343
423-842-4177

DEVONIA ANTIQUES FOR DINING
15 Charles Street
Boston, MA 01915
561-429-8566
617-523-8313
-and-
3703A S. Dixie Highway
West Palm Beach, FL 33405
www.devonia-antiques.com

FINLEY HOUSE ANTIQUES
1121 Main Street
Blowing Rock, NC 28605
828-295-6373

KNICK KNACK PADDYWHACK
ANTIQUES
1902 Stone Street
Raleigh, NC 27608
919-880-4486
knickknackpaddywhack@wordpress.com

METROLINA ANTIQUE FAIR
7100 Statesville Road
Charlotte, NC 28269
704-596-4650

MOLLY AND ME ANTIQUES
892 Main Street
Hayesville, NC 28904
828-361-3364

PORTOBELLO MARKET
288 Portobello Road
London W10 United Kingdom
01144-20-7229-8354
www.portobelloroad.co.uk

SCOTT ANTIQUE MARKET
3650 Jonesboro Road, SE
Atlanta, GA 30354
www.scottantiquemarket.com

THE STALLS
116 Bennett Street, NW
Atlanta, GA 30309
www.thestalls.com

STATUS SYMBOL ANTIQUES
110 Hexham Drive
Lynchburg, VA 24502
434-237-8500

STUF ANTIQUES
52 Broadway Street
Asheville, NC 28801
828-254-4054

VILLAGE ANTIQUES
755 Biltmore Avenue
Asheville, NC 28803
828-252-5090
www.villageantiquesonline.com

VIVIANNE METZGER ANTIQUES
31 Canoe Point
Cashiers, NC 28717

WIND ROSE
701 Hill Street
Greensboro, NC 27408
336-273-2424
www.thewindrose.net

FURNITURE AND ACCESSORIES

BAKER FURNITURE COMPANY
1170 Bugle Lane
Hickory, NC 28601
828-624-7000

THE CHARLES STEWART COMPANY
931 18th Street Place NW
Hickory, NC 28601-3347
828-322-9694

CURRIN (FURNITURE)
503 Aztec Drive
Archdale, NC 27263
336-434-5909
www.crcurrin.com

FIRST CIRCLE
218 NE 38th Street
Oklahoma City, OK 73105
405-528-2828
www.firstcircle.com

HICKORY CHAIR FURNITURE COMPANY
37 9th Street Place
Hickory, NC 28603-2147
800-785-4579
www.hickorychair.com

JAN SHOWERS
1308 Slocum Street
Dallas, TX 75207
214-747-5252

NEW MORNING GALLERY
7 Boston Way
Asheville, NC 28803
828-274-2831
www.newmorninggallerync.com

NEW RIVER ARTISANS, INC.
528 Piney Creek School Road
Piney Creek, NC 28663
336-359-2216
www.newriverartisans.com

KATHRYN GREELEY DESIGNS
619 South Haywood Street
Waynesville, NC 28786
828-452-2093
www.kathryngreeleydesigns.com

PIEPER GLASS
Kenny Pieper
2778 Halls Chapel Road
Burnsville, NC 28714
828-675-1113
www.pieperglass.com

TOMMY MITCHELL COMPANY
814 Old Mill Road
Chapel Hill, NC 27514
919-933-3183
www.tommymitchellcompany.com

FOOD

BLUE RIDGE BAKING COMPANY
Waynesville, NC 29786
828-400-5795

THE CHOCOLATE FETISH
36 Haywood Street
Asheville, NC 28801
www.chocolatefetish.com

THE CLASSIC WINE SELLER, INC.
20 Church Street
Waynesville, NC 28786
828-452-6000
www.classicwineseller.com

DARK COVE FARMS
Cullowhee, NC 28723
828-293-3791
www.darkcove.com

SUNBURST TROUT COMPANY
128 Raceway Place
Canton, NC 28716
828-648-3010
www.sunbursttrout.com

FAVORS AND INVITATIONS

THE BAGGIE GOOSE
3 Swan Street
Asheville, NC 28803
828-274-3333
www.thebaggiegoose.com

CHELSEA'S TEA ROOM
6 Boston Way
Asheville, NC 28803
828-274-4400
www.chelseastea.com

THE GARDENER'S COTTAGE
34 All Souls Crescent
Asheville, NC 28803
828-277-2020
www.gardenerscottagebiltmore.com

THE HAZELWOOD SOAP COMPANY
452 Hazelwood Avenue
Waynesville, NC 28786
828-456-3385
www.hazelwoodsoapcompany.com

TABLETOP SHOPS

THE MUD DABBER'S POTTERY
20767 Great Smoky Mountain Express
Balsam, NC 28707
828-456-1916
www.muddabbers.com

QUINTESSENTIALS
The Alexan at North Hills
4209 Lassiter Mill Road, Suite 119
Raleigh, NC 27609
919-785-0787
www.shopquintessentials.com

REPLACEMENTS, LTD.
1089 Knox Road
McLeansville, NC 27301
800-737-5223
www.replacements.com

THOMAS GOODE & CO.
19 South Audley Street
London WIK2BN, UK
01144-207-499-2823
www.thomasgoode.com

BEST BOOK-STORE FOR BOOKS ON HOME, GARDEN, AND ENTERTAINING

ARCHIVIA BOOKS
993 Lexington Avenue
New York, NY 10021
212-570-9565
www.archiviabooks.com

OTHER USEFUL ADDRESSES

BALLYCASTLE HOUSE (BED AND BREAKFAST)
20 Mountstewart Road
Newtownards
County Downs Northern Ireland
028-4278-8357
www.ballycastlehouse.com

BALLYMALOE COOKERY SCHOOL
Shanagarry
County Cork
Ireland
002-1464-6785
www.cookingisfun.ie.com